"Ego, si Deo annuente vita comes fuerit, eidem loco ita prospiciam, ut magis ei vini abundet copia, quam aquarum in alia praestanti abbatia."

Guiliamus I, Chronicon Monasterii de Bello

'If God spare my life I will so amply provide for this place that wine shall be more abundant here than water is in any other great Abbey.'

William I, Chronicle of Battle Abbey

The sword of Battle Abbey

KEITH D. FOORD

BATTLE ABBEY and BATTLE CHURCHES since 1066

The varied and sometimes extraordinary stories of the Churches of Battle and their founders, people and benefactors, from the Battle of Hastings through the foundation of the Abbey Church until 2011

Published by Battle Methodist Church
bmcbooks, 38 Hastings Road, Battle TN33 0TE
bmcbooks@foord.clara.co.uk

First published 2011

Copyright © Keith D. Foord under ⓒ **creative**
                                    commons

Typeface : Palatino Linotype

Printed and bound by CPI Group (UK) Ltd, Croydon CR0 4YY

A CIP catalogue record for this book is available from the British Library

Paperback ISBN 987-0-9569597-0-6

For Paula, with love

My thanks to the people of Battle Methodist Church for the inspiration to write this book and to those of the present and past Christian congregations of Battle who have contributed directly or indirectly. May their work for God and the community prosper.

Proceeds from the sale of this book will all go to the Battle Methodist Church re-location fund

Acknowledgements

My thanks to Christine and the Rev. David Freeland and Alastair Munro of Battle Methodist Church for their constant enthusiasm for this project and substantial help including editing. Val Kemm also reviewed the book prior to publication and Chris and Gareth Evans were most helpful with sorting out some problems with the images .

So much has been written about Battle over the centuries that writing a 'history' book like this means that so much information is necessarily repeated from elsewhere. Peter Coote had already trawled minutes of the Methodist Chapel from 1903 and cheerfully allowed me to use his material for Chapter 8. I have received further willing help for other Chapters. John Allen, producer of the Sussex Parish Churches website, provided advice and some text on St Mary's Church. John Southam of Battle Baptists supplied several background documents for and provided feedback from both himself and the Rev. Denis Nolan on Chapters 5, 6 and 7. Denis Nolan had already published some on-line history extracts about the Baptist Church which also gave useful pointers. Julia Thorp of the Church of the Ascension at Telham provided me with the excellent leaflet on that Church written by Alec Carter in 2001 and which informed the basis of Chapter 11. Christine Hughes provided a copy of Fr. Terence McLean Wilson's detailed typescript about the Catholic Parish of Battle and Northiam and commented on the chapter about the Roman Catholic Church and Rhod Jones of the Ashburnham Christian Trust also kindly commented on the Ashburnham issues. My old neighbour, David Jenner, to my great surprise, had in his personal possession some documents concerning the Congregational Church and his great grandfather's involvement in its foundation. He willingly passed these to me to study and they have now been passed on to the East Sussex Record Office (ESRO) for safe-keeping. The academic works about Battle Abbey and its Banlieu by the late Prof. Eleanor Searle have been drawn on heavily for the early chapters.

The staff of Battle Library , ESRO and Alison McCann of WSRO are all thanked. British History On-line and the National Archives (A2A) are both invaluable and 'Internet Archive' and 'Google Books' give access to down-loadable long out of date books which are a treasury of information (which is sometimes dubious, at other times in Latin and sometimes both!). ESRO kindly gave permission for images from their archives to be reproduced.

Keith D. Foord, Battle, 2011

Contents in Chronological Order

List of Grey-scale Figures

List of Colour Plates

Measurements

Throughout this book measurements are given wherever possible in metric units, with old non-metric and ancient equivalents given in brackets. Some conversions and explanations are given below.

Length

1 metre = 1.094 yards or 3.281 feet: 1 foot = 0.305 m: 1 yard = 0.914 m
1 kilometre = 0.621 miles: 1 mile = 1.609 kilometres:
16½ feet = 1 perch: 40 perches = 1 rood :
1 English league = 12 roods = 1.5 miles = 2.41 kilometres

Area

1 sq. kilometre = 0.386 sq. miles: 1 sq. mile = 2.590 sq. kilometres
1 hectare = 1/100th of a sq. km = 2.471 acres: 1 acre = 0.405Ha
1 virgate or wist = 32 acres: 1 hide = 8 virgates or wists. *Of uncleared land. This seemed to be a local Battle Abbey variation to encourage land clearance. After clearance and in use 1 hide = 4 virgates*

Money

The British pound before 1971 was divided into 20 shillings (s) with each shilling divided into 12 old pence (d = denarius, a Latin word), i.e. there were 240 d(enarii) in each pound[1]. Each d. was divided into 4 farthings. There are now 100 pence (p) to each pound.
1 s   = 5 pence:
1 d   = just over 0.4 p:
The Mark was never a coin, only an accounting unit.
1 mark = 13 s and 4 d (i.e. ⅔ of one pound or 66.67 p).

---

1   This was because originally 240 silver pennies (denarii) weighed one troy pound. To confuse further there are only 12 troy ounces to each troy pound. Troy ounces are heavier (but not proportionately) than the old avoirdupois ounces, 16 of which make up the avoirdupois pound which was used in the UK for weighing goods pre metrication. So a troy pound (at 373 grams) is lighter than the pound previously used for greengroceries (which is 453 grams). The troy system is believed to have derived in ancient times from the city of Troyes in France.

Chapter 1

An Introduction to the Banlieu of Battle Abbey 1066 to date

In 1070 five Benedictine monks in their black robes finished their long journey from the Abbey of Saint Martin of Tours, at Marmoutier on the Loire in France, by climbing up a long sandy scrubby slope to the top of a ridge in Sussex, England.

When they reached the top they found a marker. This was the point where Harold, the last Saxon king of England had fallen four years before in 1066. Twenty years after 1066 this place would be called Labatailge or La Batailge in the Domesday book.

The Blackfriars had orders from William the Conqueror to found the Abbey Church of the Holy and indivisible Trinity and the blessed Mary, forever virgin also the blessed Martin, confessor of Christ, with its high altar on the spot where Harold Godwinson fell. They must have built huts and a small chapel for themselves soon after they arrived and since this chapel was built churches have existed in Battle.

The monks started from absolutely nothing on a difficult and almost uninhabited site, which must have appeared something like parts of Ashdown Forest today. Construction of the Abbey Church was slow and they had to recruit craftsmen and helpers from neighbouring counties and from further afield including from mainland Europe.

It was not until 1076 that the first small part could be consecrated. The final consecration of the Abbey Church was nearly 20 years later in 1095, after the death of the Conqueror. The service was attended by King William II (Rufus), William the Conqueror's son, together with Archbishop Anselm of Canterbury and seven other Bishops.

Most of the Abbey was constructed of locally quarried sandstone with some Caen stone used for special features. Later some Purbeck and Sussex 'marble' or polished limestone was used in the cloisters. The Abbey was extended to the east in the 14th century making it nearly 50% larger.

To help provide for its upkeep Battle Abbey was given a *'Banlieu'* of land, one league[1] in radius from its high altar, as well as other estates. The Banlieu as described in the 'Chronicle of Battle Abbey' (Fig. A1) was truly circular (Fig.A2) and is described as:

'From without Bodehurst[2], near the land of Robert Bos and it runs near the land of Roger Moin as far as Hecilande[3] and includes Heciland near the land of William Fitz-Robert-Fitz-Waldo and the land of Croherste[4] on the south. Thence it passes by the land of Cattesfelde[5] and by Puchehole[6] as far as Westbece[7] near the land of Bodeham[8] to the west. After this it passes along by the land of Itintune[9] as far as the north. Thence there is a boundary by the land of Wetlingetuna[10] and the land of Wicham[11] and by Setlescombe[12] and thus it returns to the first limit, namely without Bodehurst on the east.'

What confuses the later descriptions of the Banlieu is that the Abbey also held local lands outside of this circle by the time the Chronicle of Battle Abbey was written in the 12th century. It had farms and smallholdings at Netherfield, Penhurst, Crowhurst, Hooe, Wilting, Hollington and Filsham and a place called Bulintune (near Bulverhythe) and a hay meadow at Bodiam. The original circle gives

---

1 An English league or leuga was defined as 12 roods, with 40 perches x 16½ feet making up a rood. This makes a league 2.41km (1 1/2 miles) although at the time the Chronicle was written the Norman (Roman) league of 2.225km may have been used. A Roman mile = 5000 feet, a Roman league = 7500feet.

2 *Bodehurst* – now Buckhurst. Battle Great Wood was called Buckhurst Wood on the O.S. Map of 1813.

3 *Hecilande* – Hedgeland (east of Telham Hill, probably the area near the Black Horse Pub.

4 *Croherste* - Crowhurst

5 *Cattesfelde* - Catsfield

6 No modern equivalent. Obviously between Catsfield and Great Beech Farm.Must have been the area of Parkgate / Great Park Farm.

7 Great Beech Farm. East Beech Farm is north of Sedlescombe

8 Landowners name, not Bodiam

9 Eatenden

10 Whatlington

11 Landowners name

12 Sedlescombe

the scope of this book which will look at both the histories of the churches which have existed within the Banlieu of Battle Abbey and at some of the people who were associated with them

The next church of Battle was started sometime after 1102, for the people of what was by then a thriving village supporting the Abbey. This was the Church of St Mary the Virgin. Founded by the Abbey 'for the people of Battell', it has seen many changes in its 900 year existence. This church has been the establishment Church of Battle, firstly Catholic and then after the Reformation, Church of England.

It was the only church for centuries, but after the Commonwealth of Oliver Cromwell which unleashed a time of change its position was slowly challenged. In the last decade of the 17th century Presbyterianism came to Battle. Presbyterianism, which had been adopted by England as its state church during the Commonwealth, did not die out on the restoration of the monarchy, as its temporary adoption had led to a more general popularisation of radical Protestantism.

Presbyterianism was taken up in Battle from about 1698 with about 120 adherents by 1715, but the numbers attending diminished slowly until about 1772 when it seemed to disappear. This was because of the emergence of varying new strands of Non-conformity.

At first post-Presbyterian Non-conformity in Battle was taken forwards by the Independent Calvinists (1776-1782), who became Independent Calvinist Baptists (1782-1793). They bought the old Presbyterian house and part of an orchard on Mount Street in 1782. They then pulled down the old meeting house and rebuilt a new chapel in 1790. This chapel had a graveyard and this burial ground would be of some importance in the 20th century.

By the late 18th/early 19th century some 50% of the Christians of Battle were Non-conformists. But radical challenges continued. The Baptists split with some apparent rancour in 1793 into Universalists (who then became Unitarians) and Zion Particular Baptists, now Battle Baptists. The Unitarians kept the old chapel.

The other group, the Particular Baptists, first worshipped in houses then were leased some land and built a wooden chapel circa. 1786 and finally the Zion Chapel in 1820 which became the Battle Baptist base. This has 1990 and 2002 extensions with another smaller

4

extension in 2011. The Unitarians and Baptists were uncomfortably next door to each other on Mount Street. But in its turn the Unitarian Chapel building (the 1790 one), was not needed after 1898 as Unitarianism waned and died out in Battle. It was used as an educational institute and then a store. It was finally demolished in 1957. The story of the site after that is interesting as will be seen in later chapters.

Battle Wesleyan Methodists were founded about 1804, with their first minister coming from the Zion Particular Baptists. They rented rooms at first and their Chapel on Lower Lake was not built until 1826. In 1887 it had a porch added at the front and a large house built on it to the rear. They are now to be housed in their new Church at Blackfriars, off Marley Lane. Their old Chapel which is a Grade II listed building is being redeveloped.

In common with the maelstrom of radical Protestantism occurring all over Britain multiple other small dissenting groups were to be founded in Battle in the 19th century. The most notable were the Strict Baptists who met in an upper room of the Langton Hall from 1870-1920. They never had their own building. There were other Dissenters, who had a House registered at Whatlington in 1813 plus a building in the High Street, Battle (registered for worship 1820), Free Thinking Christians (registered for worship 1829), Protestant Dissenters in a house on Battle Hill (registered for worship 1835) and other Protestant Dissenters in a house near the Watch Oak (also registered for worship 1835).

Another, this time Victorian, Church of England Chapel was built at Telham from 1876 at the expense of the then Dean of Battle, the Very Reverend Edward Neville Crake, on land given by Sir Archibald Lamb. This is now called the Church of the Ascension (1877 to date), but was originally called the Mission Chapel of the Ascension.

This was followed by a Congregational Chapel (1881 – closed about 1950) on the High Street and the Roman Catholic Church of Our Lady Immaculate and Saint Michael (1882 / 85 to date) which was funded by the 5th Earl of Ashburnham, with some apparent local opposition, in the grounds of a house off Mount Street beside the Zion Chapel.....not that Catholicism had completely disappeared from the Battle area after the Reformation as we shall see later.

So the new Methodist Church and Community Centre is the first new whole church to be built within the Battle banlieu for 129 years.

This is an ecumenical book, written from multiple sources which are listed at the end – the reader is warned that some sources may be more than a little suspect, written many years away from the events they describe or written from biased viewpoints.

It must obviously also be an abridged history, with salient facts taken from many works, some of which are superbly detailed and researched. The author cannot hope to emulate these latter towers of scholarship, only admire the years of work reading and interpreting handwritten manuscripts in Latin that they must represent.

Where possible the facts are objectively adhered to and when a point of view is suspect this is pointed out, but the author is not a professional historian and confesses that any errors of interpretation must be his.

Chapter 2

The Abbey Church of the Holy and indivisible Trinity and the blessed Mary, forever virgin also the blessed Martin, confessor of Christ *or* 'The Church of the Abbey of St. Martin at Battle' – 'Abbatia Sancti Martini de Labatailge' 1070 – 1538

Figure 1. Battle Abbey Gatehouse 1818

The battlefield of 1066 still has one of the most impressive monuments to victory. Battle Abbey's gatehouse (Fig.1) is the signature mark of Battle and dominates its High Street and Abbey Green, seeming to bar the way as it is approached from the north.

Sadly, beyond the gate, there is very little today of the Abbey Church, which was demolished after 1538. There are only a few visible foundations to be seen, so it is very difficult to visualise exactly how it appeared in its four and a half centuries of existence. A visit is to be recommended to view the other ruins which have not been razed and to drink in the atmosphere of what remains and the vista of the battlefield of 14th October 1066. Those from the English speaking world may do this with some emotion. Viewing the land which falls away from the Abbey and realising the strength of Harold Godwinson's position that day, on the ridges above William, Duke of Normandy it is possible to understand that the battle was a close run thing. If it had gone the other way English as a language may not have evolved and the history of the English speaking world would not have existed, or if so neither exactly in the ways they happened. And on very much smaller planes the Abbey Church would not have been built and this book would not exist.

Browne-Willis in his 'History of Mitred[13] Abbeys, 1718' says."*Though this Abbey be demolished, yet the magnificence of it appears by the ruins of the cloisters, &c, and by the largeness of the hall, kitchen, and gate-house, of which the last is entirely preserved. It is a noble pile....*" The Abbey Church was built in the 11th century and extended in the 14th century. It stood for over 450 years until it was razed to the ground after 1538, at the time of the dissolution of the monasteries in the reign of Henry VIII. The earliest authentic record about Battle Abbey is in the Anglo-Saxon Chronicle. ' *King William built a noble monastery on the spot where God allowed him to conquer England, that he put monks therein and made them rich.*' Its heraldic arms varied down the ages and some are depicted in Figure A3.

Few remains of the actual Abbey Church have survived above ground, but excavations in the 1800s, in 1929-1934 and the latest English Heritage study of 1978-80 and some minor studies since then have revealed the foundations and the original eastern end of the church, as well as the extended eastern end of the later 14th century presbytery, apse and apsidal chapels and crypts. The Victoria County History of Sussex Vol. 9 contains excellent ground plans by Sir Harold Brakspear, not really bettered since, as shown below in Figs.2 and 10. A remnant of the SW corner also gives the information that the aisles were narrow and vaulted.

From archaeological evidence the following appears to describe the Abbey Church, which was planned to be the second longest Minster in England after Canterbury.

---

13 As a mitred Abbey the Abbot would have attended the King's court and parliament as required. The Abbot de Bello (Battle) was a witness to the signing of Magna Carta in this role. The various arms of the Abbey are given as Figure A3 in the first colour section.

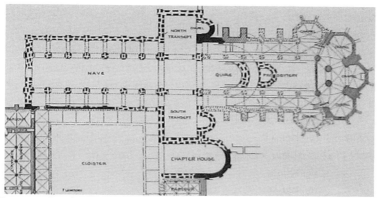

Figure 2. Brakspear's ground plan of the Abbey Church from the
Victoria County History of Sussex Vol. 9

The original church was built in the form of a cross, with three small
apsidal chapels at its eastern end representing a simple crown set so
that one pointed north-east, one east and the last south-east in a
trefoil. There was an ambulatory around the apse allowing access to
these chapels. This was a new feature in abbey church architecture,
borrowed directly from the ancient Church of St Martin at Tours[14]
and also used for abbeys in the Loire.

The overall length of the original church was 68 m (224 feet) and it
was 19 m (62 feet)) wide, with a transept 10.6 m (35 feet) wide. Each
transept was about 9.5 m deep and had a small rounded chapel on its
eastern side. The nave was nearly 40m (130 feet) long, so the
presbytery and apse was quite short at 18 m (59 feet). The apse was
rounded as is clear from the foundation plans. In addition there were
three small rounded apsidal chapels.

The features above ground can only be surmised, but reference to
other Benedictine Abbeys of France from about this date, particularly
the Abbaye de Lessay (Fig.A4) and the early parts of the Abbaye aux
Hommes, Caen (Figs. A5 and A6) suggests relatively simple
structures for the early 11th century building.

---

14 This was a different secular church from the Abbey of Marmoutier. The
    secular church with its tomb of St. Martin was within Tours itself, now the
    site of a basilica. Marmoutier is on the opposite north bank of the Loire, east
    of the present A10 autoroute, further to the east of the city centre.

The illustration below (Fig.3) is based on the ground plans of Battle Abbey Church as in the 11th century and the fact that early Benedictine Abbey Churches were quite plain. A 'best guess' has been applied to the drawing which is not claimed to be definitive .

Figure 3. Possible elevations of the 11c. Abbey Church, clockwise West to South from top left

The Church was extended in the 14th century. The inspiration for the eastern extension of the Abbey Church is said to have been the new Westminster Abbey with its early Gothic features. The final length was reckoned to have become just over 96 metres (316 ft), made up of the unaltered nave and transepts, but with the choir and presbytery extended to 32.6 m (107 ft) and the crypt ambulatory and the now five hemi-octagonal apse chapels at least three of which were crypt chapels adding another 13.4 m (44 ft). In addition at the position of the two side apsidal chapels the width had increased to 24 metres (79 feet) whereas the rest of the Church was only the original 19 metres (62 feet) wide.

The new features at the apse were buttresses and two side apsidal chapels as well as vaulted crypts underneath the presbytery and the three eastern crypt apsidal chapels, accessed by stairs from the choir side aisles. These would have made an extension easier to build on the sloping site as an extension without these would have entailed considerable earth and rock importation. The next drawing below (Fig.4) shows possible elevations of the Abbey Church after this work which created a chevet.

The Church was not quite aligned west-east with the altar at the eastern end, but examination of the ground contours during the English Heritage survey of 1978-80 showed that the alignment does follow the contours as near east-west as would have been possible, without having to massively build up land to the north-west and south-east. The major difficulty would have been in placing the high altar on the 'exact' site of Harold's demise, which would have constrained the Church position. As can be seen the incorporation of crypts under the apse (Figs.5, A7 and A8) aided the later eastward extension.

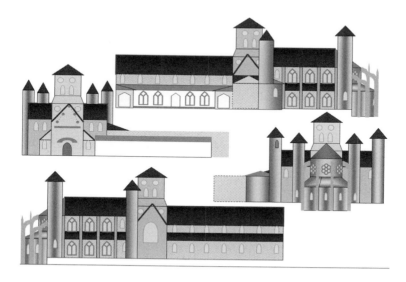

Figure 4. Possible elevations of the 14th c. Abbey Church.

The three early chapels (or perhaps two with the short choir) with tiled roofs are shown in side perspective on an early seal (Fig. 6) which also shows the clerestory nave with its covered side aisles. The other later seal (Fig. 7) clearly shows a clerestory of round headed windows and what appear to be tiered towers at the ends of the transepts. At the west end appears a large gable with rounded windows over a large arch. The central tower on both seals has a low tiled pyramidal roof with round headed windows under circular windows.

Figure 5. A piscina in an Abbey Church crypt chapel

Figure 6. An early seal

Figure 7. A later, possibly the final seal

It is difficult to explain the two towers behind the transepts on the second seal, unless there was a tower over each transept chapel and/or the first and fifth apsidal chapels and/or until it is realised that there was at least one separate bell tower, with a rounded or polygonal base 9 m (28 feet) in diameter south-east of the southern-most apsidal chapel (its base is clearly shown on early OS maps and in www.battle-abbey.co.uk) . This area is now exactly where there are several large trees. The position of the bell tower is shown in Fig. 8. Perhaps (although unlikely) there was a mirrored second bell tower to the north or artistic licence has been used to balance the look of the seal. The author chanced upon an internet item that suggested the bells may have been called Mary and Gabriel[15]. The seal maker must also have rotated the nave with its clerestory as the transepts were narrow (only 10.5 m wide) and there are no supporting pillars for a stone clerestory – so the maker of the seals may have used Picasso-esque distortions for his representations.

Where did the transept towers on the later seal appear from? There is no sign of these on the early seal, but Brakspear and then Helm report that there is a suspicion of foundations at the NE and SE corners of the transepts. These may have been small as are seen at the Abbaye aux Hommes (Fig A5) which was also built on the orders of William I. We would be foolish to interpret too much from the

---

15   Ædric the bellmaker lived at messuage 38 almost opposite the Abbey
      between 1102-1107 (Chronicle of Battle Abbey)

14

seals however, as they may exaggerate features and are scant and probably inaccurate evidence.

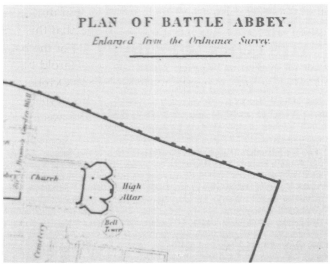

Figure 8. The position of the Abbey Church Bell Tower

Excluding the Abbey Church the remains of the Abbey that can be seen today are the 13th century dormitory, the vaults beneath the guest house, some remains of the west side of the cloister, the gate house and the protective walls. The gate house itself is one of the best surviving medieval monastic gate houses in Britain, although the earliest part is incorporated in its western end it also had later 14th century additions, plus a 16th century court-house which was attached to its northern side. So the other buildings that can still be seen have nothing to do with the Church building itself (see Fig. 10), although the eastern cloister walls can still be seen incorporated in the wall to the 16th century house built by Sir Anthony Browne (see photograph of the eastern side of the manor house Fig.9), which also incorporated the Abbot's house and great hall, using the stones of the Abbey Church.

The story of the foundation of the Abbey has two versions. One or neither may be true. The first is that William, Duke of Normandy, vowed on the eve of the battle that if God gave him success he would found a monastery upon the place of victory. The second is that Pope Alexander II on confirming the coronation of William I in 1070 demanded that William do penance for the English and Norman lives lost, not just on the battlefield of Hastings, but during the truly bloody progress of the Conquest after that – and that this was when the vow was made to build the Abbey on the site of the battle, with the high altar of its Church at the place where Harold had not just fallen, but was hacked to pieces on Saturday 14th October 1066. The second explanation seems more likely as thoughts of the future must have been far from William's mind when the battle was imminent.

Figure 9. The eastern cloister wall incorporated in the later house

The task of supervising the construction of the Abbey was given to the Benedictine Abbey of Saint Martin of Tours at Marmoutier, near Tours on the Loire (not to be confused with Marmoutiers in Alsace). This Abbey had been founded by St. Martin in late Roman Gaul in 372 and had itself been raided and pillaged by early Normans in 835, but had recovered and become one of the richest abbeys in Europe. Poignantly it too was demolished in 1819 at the time of the French Revolution. A convent built a new chapel there in 1856 and established a school which still exists. Part of the site of the ruins belongs to the City of Tours and is under archaeological study.

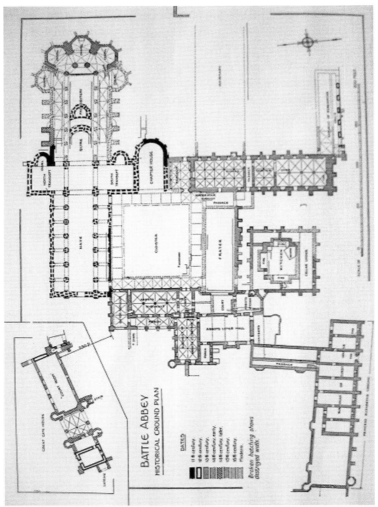

Figure 10. Sir Harold Brakspear's plan of the whole Abbey site (Victoria County History of Sussex Vol. 9)

William sent William Faber 'the Smith', a monk in his service, to Marmoutier and he and four other monks, Theobald 'the old', William Coche, Robert of Boulogne and Robert Blancard returned to start the new community. However when the five saw the constricted site which was on top of a dry scrubby sandstone ridge, much as in Ashdown Forest today (Fig.11) with no nearby water supply[16] and surrounded by waterlogged heavy clay valleys and the dense Wealden Forest, which was only sparsely inhabited, they considered it unsuitable and tried to build it further to the west at a place called Herst (possibly in the area of the present Asten Fields).

Figure 11. The ridge at Battle must have appeared something like this photo of Ashdown Forest scrub and trees when the four monks arrived © Malc McDonald. Licensed for reuse under a Creative Commons Licence

Apparently when William I was informed of this they were told in no uncertain terms to build it where they were told to. Upon the monks pleading a scarcity of water at the site he is said to have replied,

---

16 There is in fact a small spring south east of the eastern end of the Abbey Church ruins which later fed a small fishpond.

'If God spare my life I will so amply provide for this place that wine shall be more abundant here than water is in any other great abbey.'

The Abbey was built mainly of locally quarried stone, again after complaints from the monks that they would like Caen stone. Some Caen limestone was imported and used for the more decorative stonework for which the local sandstone would have been unsuitable. Local sandstone is very friable, but there is a blue-stone variety which hardens after quarrying and cutting and this must have been extensively used. There are several old quarries around the area of the old Great Park[17], but the nearest quarry is described to the east south east of the Church itself, which would place it near the top end of the present Lower Lake. Later still Purbeck and Sussex polished limestone was used in the cloister.

The Chronicle of Battle Abbey states that the dedication of the abbey was to the Holy and indivisible Trinity and the blessed Mary, forever virgin also the blessed Martin, confessor of Christ. As William 'the Smith' is said to have suggested the name this must be the same Saint Martin of Tours who was a Roman soldier in Gaul. He converted to Christianity and became Bishop of Tours in 372 and became known as the Apostle of Gaul. Confusingly there is also a Saint Martin the Confessor who was the last Pope of Rome to be martyred in order to preserve the divinity of Christ against the Monothelite heresy. He died in 655 and was clearly not the same person as Saint Martin of Tours. The fact that William I regarded St Martin of Tours as 'his' saint, as did many Norman soldiers and that the founding monks of Battle Abbey came from the Abbey of St Martin of Tours must confirm the dedication to be truly to St Martin of Tours, but it is the word 'confessor' which leads to brief minor disquiet.

The monks at Battle Abbey, as at Marmoutier, were Blackfriars and wore the black habit of the Order of Saint Benedict, who had originally established the Benedictine rules for the monks of his own Abbey at Monte Cassino in Italy in about 540 AD. According to the Rule they took a vow of obedience, to lead a simple and self-denying

---

17 The Abbey Great Park stretched from the Abbey gate to Park Gate, near Catsfield to the west

Battle Abbey

Figures A1a and A1b

Illustrated pages from the Chronicle of Battle Abbey.

The top left illustration shows the Conqueror on his throne

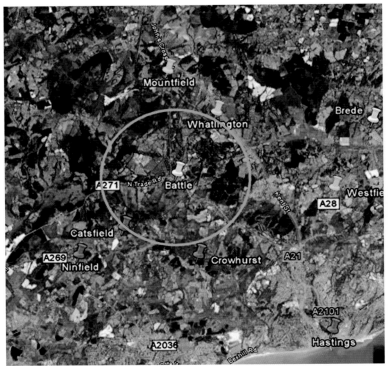

Figure A2. The green ring shows the Banlieu of Battle Abbey superimposed on a modern Google Earth satellite image.

Figure A3. Arms of Battle Abbey from various descriptions.

The second from right is the most like the arms embossed on the pommel of the Sword of Battle Abbey (centre). This sword was made during the Abbacy of Thomas of Ludlow (1417-34) – note his initials on each side of the shield (t l) - this is now in the National Museum of Scotland. The arms on the final Abbot's seal were similar except that the two swords were replaced by additional crowns The first on the left was used on Goss china mementoes of Battle.

Figure A4. Abbaye de Lessay c.1064. An early Norman Abbey

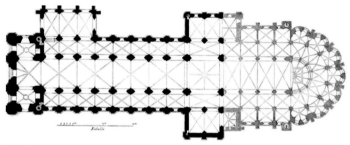

Figure A5. Ground plan of the Abbaye aux Hommes, Caen. As at Battle the complex eastern end is later in date

Figure A6. The Abbaye aux Hommes today, rather more complex than Battle Abbey would have been but showing the rounded apse with rose windows and buttressing

Figure A7. A Google Earth satellite image showing the outline of the 11th C. extent of the eastern end and three of the apsidal crypt chapels of the 14th C. extension.

The Chapter House base and the cloister rectangle are also shown. The Bell Tower would have stood bottom right.

Figure A8. The apsidal crypt chapels as they appear on the ground today

life, be celibate and own no property. The simple celebration of the daily services in praise of God was their first duty. Work and reading took up the rest of their time.

The Abbot of Marmoutier made an early attempt to make the Abbot of St. Martin at Battle go to Marmoutier to be consecrated and hence subservient to it. But William had made it very clear from the start by making the Abbey a Royal Peculiar that he wished to emphasise that in no way was his abbey to be beholden to any one else but the monarch and he ordered Marmoutier to desist from this claim.

In order to fund and finance the new Abbey William bestowed his foundation with all the land within a radius of a league (the banlieu or leuga or lowey), the estate of Alciston in Sussex, the royal manor of Wye in Kent with its lands of Dungemarsh on the coast (this amounted to about 20% of Kent according to Lambarde), Limpsfield in Surrey, Hoo in Essex, Brightwalton in Berkshire, Crowmarsh in Oxfordshire,and churches in Reading, Cullompton and Exeter. Rather more extraordinarily, William had declared that the Abbey was to be a 'Royal Peculiar' of the same status as Canterbury and that within its banlieu the rule of Abbot was to be absolute. Bishops and royal officers could not interfere there and taxes and other dues were not levied.

The banlieu of the Abbey is mentioned in the Domesday book of 1086 variously as 'Sancti Martini de Labatailge' or 'Abbatia Sancti Martini de loco belli' or 'Æcclesia de la Batailge', but the area around was 'part of the hundred of 'Hailesaltede' still of little value at that time, what little there was having been 'wasted' in 1066. In fact the only 'populous' area of the hundred was to the north with households numbering 4 at Uckham, 11 at Mountfield, 13 at Netherfield and 12 at Brightling. Battle itself was recorded as zero....this may have been a 'zero return' as the banlieu was also recorded as being under the sole control of the Abbot with 32 peasant holdings. The developing village was counted as having 21 'bordars'[18]. The only areas nearby with any significant populations were around the lower lying coastal areas of the Coombe Haven at

---

18   A bordar ranked below a serf in the social hierarchy of a manor, holding a cottage, garden and just enough land to feed a family . The Battle Abbey messuages were of about this size with long thin gardens.

Filsham (89 households), Crowhurst(22), Wilting (14), Cortesley[19](27) and Hooe(73). These coastal zones would have been much easier to farm. However Domesday did record that the gross income of the Abbey was £212 3s 2d, the largest income of any religious house in England and larger than the English income of the Abbaye de Fécamp (which held adjacent lands around Brede and Rye) or any other Norman abbey. But in terms of overall wealth it stood at 'only' 15th.

Fifty years later in 1124 there were about 5.7 km^2 (1400 acres) in agricultural use around the Abbey with controlled hereditary tenancies. But the Abbey tightly controlled immigration to the town of Battle by 'vetting' individual's usefulness to the Abbey. It was also buying land around the banlieu with its profits and this was rented. It also had a few boundary disputes with other local landowners, usually settled by exchanges of land.

The Abbey was 'mitred' which meant that the Abbot was required to attend the King's court and parliament when summoned. This is covered in the directive by William I dated 1070-1, when he mentions the Abbot of Battle[20]. When the Abbot was called to attend the King's court he had an allowance of food, wine, and wax candles for himself and two monks. From 1295 he was granted a residence in both London, the 'Inne of Bataille' in Southwark near the present Hays Wharf, and also in Winchester, but perhaps the most clear privilege was that the Abbot when passing through the king's forests might hunt one or two game animals with his hounds.

The building progressed slowly and it may not have been until 1076 that the first Abbot was appointed. Robert Blancard, one of the four monks who had first come over, was elected, but coming back from Marmoutier he was drowned. After this Gausbert was fetched from Marmoutier with four more Blackfriars and was consecrated Abbot.

At first Stigand, Bishop of Chichester, tried to compel Abbot Gausbert to go to Chichester for consecration, but the king commanded that the consecration should be in the Abbey Church

---

19 Cortesley is shown as west of Filsham between it and Bulverhythe
20 William 1 may have designated Robert Blancard as Abbot from 1070-1, not
    1076, but perhaps he could not be formally appointed until the Abbey
    Church was first consecrated in 1076 ?(See page 1)

itself. The Abbey was not to be beholden to Chichester although it lay in that Diocese. This would become an ongoing issue over the next few centuries.

When the Conqueror died he is recorded as bequeathing to his Abbey his royal embroidered cloak, a splendid collection of relics, and a portable altar containing relics, possibly the identical one on which Harold had sworn his famous oath as depicted in the Bayeux Tapestry. William II (Rufus) further added the Monastery of Bromham in Wiltshire to the Abbey's land possessions.

In February, 1095 the Abbey Church was at last consecrated in the presence of William II Rufus, Archbishop Anselm of Canterbury and Bishops Walchelin of Winchester, Ralph of Chichester, Osmund of Salisbury, John of Bath, William of Durham, Roger of Coutances and Gundalf of Rochester.

At this time Rufus gave the Abbey yet another nine churches and twelve dependent chapels in Norfolk, Suffolk, and Essex to add to their estates. However the Abbey was still not completely finished as the roof was leaded during the next Abbacy.

Although the Abbey had a considerable number of English and Welsh churches in its gift, its Sussex patronage was surprisingly small, consisting only of Alciston with the chapel of Lullington, until in Henry I's reign the Church of Westfield, with a wist of land and even a pit for the ordeal by water was added. The Church of Icklesham was given by Nicholas Haringod in 1226, and the Chapel of Whatlington by Simon de Etchingham.

The income of the Abbey was further increased by gifts, purchases and exchange, as Henry I, wishing to found a monastery at Reading, gave the Abbey of Battle the manors of Funtington and Appledram near Chichester in exchange for Battle's Reading estate. The complete list of endowments and their dates are recorded in the Chronicles of Battle Abbey. By 1291 the property of the Abbey was valued at £528 10s, of which £211 came from Sussex[21].

Abbot Gausbert died in July, 1095, soon after the consecration of the Abbey Church. The monks applied to the king for permission to elect a fresh head, who should, in accordance with their charter, be one of

---

21 The conversion level in 2011 cf. 1300 is a factor of approximately 10,000x. So the Abbey property would have been worth approx. £5M at 2011 value.

their own number. William II delayed for some time, but at last following the advice of Archbishop Anselm promoted Henry, prior of Christ Church, Canterbury, in June 1096. Henry made the mistake of allowing Bishop Ralph to consecrate him at Chichester and this was a lever by which Ralph tried to make the Abbey responsible to the Diocese.

In 1101 Henry I, who was camped a short distance away at Wartling expecting an invasion of Norman barons, strengthened the Abbey's court and standing considerably with a declaration that within the banlieu the Abbot's court should be the first to hear any legal cases[22].

For a while after the death of Abbot Henry in 1102 the Abbey was managed by various clerks, but in 1107 King Henry I appointed Ralph, Prior of Rochester, to the long-vacant abbacy. He proved a good Abbot and excellent relations were established with his namesake at Chichester, who finally accepted the exemption of the Abbey and also the parish church of Battle from his control.

It was either the monks in the period of the vacancy 1102-1107 or Abbot Ralph immediately after his appointment who decided to build the parish church outside of the Abbey walls for the people of Battle, who had grown in number in order to service the needs of the Abbey. Probably the local people were overcrowding the nave of the Abbey church and interfering with the Abbey's Benedictine religious duties.

Ralph died in 1124, and was succeeded by Warner, a monk of Canterbury. He somehow offended King Stephen probably by supporting Empress Matilda and resigned his abbacy and retired to the Cluniac Priory of Lewes. The resignation may have been manipulated by Richard de Luci as he was followed in 1139 by Walter de Luci, brother of Richard who was the Chief Justiciar.

Thanks to his powerful connections Walter de Luci advanced the

---

22 William I had bequeathed Normandy to his son Robert and England to William II Rufus. This divided the loyalty of the great Barons who held lands on both sides of the Channel. Only one of the five Rapes of Sussex was held by a Baron loyal to Rufus. Henry I succeeded William II in 1100 and expected an invasion challenge by his uncle from Normandy. Eventually Henry I defeated Robert in Normandy in 1106 at the Battle of Tinchebrai and Normandy and England were re-united. It suited Henry I well to have part of Hastings Rape held by the Abbey.

prosperity of the abbey, recovering estates which had been 'borrowed'. He supervised the construction of a cloister[23] using Sussex and Purbeck marble (polished limestone). Once more, with his brother's help, he needed to get confirmation of the Abbey's charters and Royal Peculiar status from Henry II . On his death in 1171 his brother placed the the Abbey in the hands of Sir Peter de Criel and Hugh de Beche, who managed its affairs during a four years' vacancy.

In 1175, the king agreed to nominate Odo, Prior of Canterbury, as Abbot, but Odo himself refused the honour, appealing to the pope and even offering to resign his prior-ship rather than be Abbot, but at last, fearing that he might be refusing the call of God, he unwillingly agreed. Again another Bishop of Chichester tried to interfere, but this time the consecration was performed by the Archbishop of Canterbury at South Malling. Odo proved his reputation and in 1184 was chosen to be Archbishop of Canterbury, but was rejected by the king. In March 1200 Odo was succeeded as Abbot by John of Dover.

During the rule of King John the Abbey was visited by the monarch no less than four times. He gave it a fragment of the Holy Sepulchre brought from Palestine by King Richard I. True to form in 1211 he extracted the then huge sum of 1500 Marks (£1000) from the Abbey to confirm that during an Abbatical vacancy the Abbey could look after its own affairs and also choose their new Abbot themselves[24]. While at the Abbey in 1213 he annulled his previous sentences of outlawry against some ecclesiastics and undertook never again to outlaw religious clerks.

During the 13th century the monastic buildings started to be rebuilt, firstly by the dorter range[25] which still stands, then the Abbot's house and a guest house, which have been incorporated in the later manor house.

---

23 The cloister was destroyed at the Dissolution, but its west wing wall was incorporated in the manor house. See photograph, Fig.9.

24 If the monks had waited another four years the signing of Magna Carta in 1215 gave them this right anyway. One of the reasons that the Barons forced John to sign Magna Carta was that he was rather too fond of extracting monies from them under duress.

25 Dormitories

Royal visits occurred moderately frequently although were not always welcome. In 1264, when Henry III was on his way to meet the baronial army at Lewes, he repaid the monks' hospitality with extortion, blaming them for the death of his cook. He had also robbed Robertsbridge Abbey.

In the late 13th century more re-building work took place with the large eastward extension of the Abbey Church. According to English Heritage this was influenced by the new Westminster Abbey with its Early English Gothic pointed arches, ribbed vaulting, rose windows and flying buttresses.

A licence was obtained in 1338 for the construction of a battlement wall round the Abbey precincts. The gatehouse was also enlarged at this time. It is believed this was because the French were making regular heavy raids on Sussex and had severely damaged both Hastings and Rye. But this wall could not keep out the Black Death in 1350, when the Abbot died and the population of the town and Abbey fell by an estimated 50% with a fall in the prosperity of the banlieu.

The French were to cause further trouble some years after Hamo de Offynton was elected Abbot early in 1364. He obviously had some military education as well as being a monk and in 1377 he gained fame by raising a local force to defend Winchelsea against the French.

The business affairs of the Abbey were often carried out by Abbey 'civil' servants. An active and complicated local system of property development and speculation, with trading and sub-letting had evolved which boosted the Abbey manor income and by 1200 servants of the Abbey were being rewarded with tenancies of lands. The Abbot had a council of laymen and 'inquest jurors' to help him with day to day affairs, settling disputes and tenancies and leases of property within and in the neighbourhood of the banlieu. These positions were held in families for generations. Some of these 'servants', including men of the Boyes family who are distant ancestors of the author, became quite wealthy in their own right. The first William Boyes is mentioned as an intermediary in 1305 and one of the family held a similar position until the dissolution, a span of

233 years. By the end of this period the last William[26] Boyes to serve the Abbey was reckoned to be one of the most substantial men of the town at his death in 1531 and many of the family held either freehold lands or hereditary tenancies around the banlieu.

The numbers of monks at the Abbey was never as high as the 60 possibly to be increased to 140 envisaged by William I. At the time of the dissolution there were only fifteen monks and a novice besides the Abbot.

In October, 1535, Richard Layton declared to Thomas Cromwell, Henry VIII's chancellor, whom he had appointed vice-regent to manage the dissolution.

" *That the Abbot and all but two or three of his monks were guilty of unnatural crimes and traitors"*, calling the Abbot "*the veriest hayne betle and buserde and the arrantest churl"*, adding for extra flavour the sweeping condemnation, "*the black sort of devilish monks, I am sorry to know, are past amendment."*

He was equally unimpressed by the condition of the contents of the Abbey and the way in which rents had decreased over the last one hundred years. He was a known bully and blusterer and his words were ignored by Thomas Cromwell.

Abbot Hammond remained undisturbed until 27 May 1538, when he surrendered the Abbey. From 6 July 1538 he received a generous yearly pension of 100 Marks. The sixteen other monks received pensions of 10 to 4 Marks according to their seniority and other direct employees of the Abbey also received pensions.

The Abbey plate was valued at 400 Marks of which the most interesting items were the six 'magni ciphi Haraldi de mirra,' presumably once the property of Harold, the last Saxon king of England. The net annual revenues from the manor have been estimated to be £880 14s 7d (*by Dugdale*) or gross revenues of £987 0s 11¼d (*by Speed*).

The Abbey estate was passed on 15 or 18 August 1538 to Sir Anthony Browne (Figs.12 and 13), confidante and Master of the Horse to

---

26 They were not all William, some were John. Other family names were
    Richard, Ralph, Edward and Roger all of which suggest an Abbey influence.

Henry VIII in his later years. [27]

'Sir Anthony had the grant for the House and Scite of the late Monastery of Battle, for himself and heirs, by Patent, Aug. 15, 1538, 30 Hen. VIII'.

The Conqueror's cloak is said to have been removed, along with the 'Battle Abbey Roll'[28] to Cowdray. Sir Anthony Browne also became executor of Henry VIII's will and guardian to Prince Edward and Princess Elizabeth. One of the commissioners for the dissolution, Sir John Gage received the Sword of the Abbey[29], which he kept at Firle Place.

Sir Anthony Browne also received the neighbouring lands at Brede which had previously belonged to the Abbaye de Fécamp. Only four years later he also inherited the extensive Cowdray estates on the death of his half brother the Earl of Southampton.

His family history (of the Montagues of Cowdray, as his son was made Lord Montague by Mary I) can be read elsewhere, suffice it to say here that Anthony Browne was the man who , whilst he may not personally have commissioned the destruction of the Abbey[30], he used its dressed stone to make a house. Interestingly his heirs remained overtly Catholic.

---

27 See Appendix for fuller details

28   The 'Battle Abbey Roll' was supposed to be a list of all the Norman knights involved in the 1066 Conquest with William. It was believed to be a late forgery first mentioned in 1577 by Holinshed.
   In fact quite a few such lists exist, varying widely. The Roll of Battle Abbey consisted of 645 names, some duplicates. Duchesne's list, derived from a charter formerly in the Abbey, contains 405 names. One of the lists printed in Leland's Collectanea gives 498. The rhyming catalogue, printed in Brompton's Chronicle, includes 245. Monsieur de Magny's catalogue contains 425, that compiled by Monsieur Leopold Delisle, in the church at Dive, 485 and that of Guillaume le Tailleur in the *Chronicles of Normany* only 177.

29 Images of the sword are shown on the front cover and in the preface. It was made between 1417 and 1434 whilst Thomas de Lodelowe was Abbot.

30 The commissioners ordered the destruction and handed the job to one 'Gilmer' (See Appendix)

He may have somehow remained a closet Catholic. If so politics and self preservation were more important to him than his beliefs. At his death his body joined the remains of his first wife Alys in a vault in St Mary's Church - their politically correct monument can be seen there today (Fig. B17). He had left 20 pounds in his will for this tomb to be finished. It is of painted alabaster and is believed to have been made by Italian craftsmen in London and brought to Battle on a cart. The Montagues sold the estate to Sir Thomas Webster[31] in 1719. He was succeeded by his son, Sir Whistler Webster 2nd baronet (died 1779 leaving a widow but no children and he was succeeded by his brother). Battle Abbey remained in the Webster family until 1858 during which time large portions of estate land were gradually sold off and the medieval buildings fell into further ruin. In 1885 it was sold to Lord Harry Vane, later Duke of Cleveland. The Duchess of Cleveland obviously took a great interest in her historic home and produced several books about the Abbey.

Figure 12. Sir Anthony Browne (on white horse) with King Henry VIII in the etching of the Sinking of the Mary Rose

31   Sir Thomas Webster, MP and baronet (1677-1751, created a baronet 1703, baronetcy extinct 1923) married the heiress Jane Cheek (grand-daughter of a wealthy merchant, Henry Whistler, whose vast wealth she inherited in 1719). This inheritance would appear to have financed the purchase of Battle Abbey manor given the coincidence of the same date for the inheritance and purchase.

Figure 13. Sir Anthony Browne

On her death in 1901 it was bought back by Sir Augustus Webster, 7th baronet. After WW1 the house was leased to Battle Abbey School and the school continues to occupy it today.

The Webster trustees sold the estate to the government in 1976 and the battlefield and the remaining monastic structures were put under the care of English Heritage.

Abbots of Battle

*There is a mention in Regesta Regum Anglo-Normannorum Vol.1 (No.60)[32]
about an Abbot in 1070-1. Could Robert Blancard, one of the first monks,
have actually been designated by William I in 1070, not 1076, but not been
able to be formally appointed until the first part of the Abbey Church was
consecrated in 1076?*

Robert Blancard,	?designated 1070-1, appointed 1076, drowned same year
Gausbert,	appointed 1076, died 1095
Henry,	elected 1096, died 1102

*The custody of the Abbey, during the vacancy[33] which followed
Henry's death, was first conferred on one of the King's Chaplains,
named Vivian, then on a monk Geoffrey or Gausfrid of
Carileph (Calais). He does not appear to have been appointed Abbot, but it
was under his watch that the claims of Marmoutier were refuted. After
Geoffrey's untimely death at Battle the Abbot of Thorney had care of the
Monastery until Ralph of Caen became Abbot.*

Ralph of Caen,	elected 1107, died 1124
Warner,	elected 1125, resigned 1138
Walter de Luci,	appointed 1139, died 1171

*In the period 1171 to the next Abbott's election Richard de Luci 'presided'
over the Abbey which was de facto run by Sir Peter Criel and Hugh de
Beche.*

---

32 [1070-1.] **60. Notification by William I to L[anfranc] Abp. of Canterbury .
King's barons throughout England.** That the King has granted and
confirmed that the abbot of Battle come to court at Easter, Whitsuntide, and
Christmas, and have the court livery for himself and two monks, viz. two
simnel loaves of dewaine {de dominico) and other two simnel loaves de
communi, and wine ; and of fish, or whatever might be there, three dishes
for himself and three for his monks ; and two wax candles and ten candle
ends.   Witnesses : Lanfranc Abp. of Canterbury ; William fitz Osbert.

33 This was the period between 1102 and 1107 when St Mary's Church was
initiated.

Odo,	elected 1175, died 1200
John de Dubra,	elected 1200 , died 1213
Hugh	elected before June 1215, became Bishop of Carlisle 1218

After 12 June 1215 the signing of Magna Carta (which was witnessed by the Abbott of Battle) allowed free elections in the Church. Royal nomination ceased and the Abbey then elected its own Abbot and submitted his name for formal royal approval.

Richard,	elected 1218, died 1235
Ralph de Covintre,	elected 1235, last mentioned 1251
Reginald,	elected 1261, resigned 1281
Henry de Aylesford,	elected 1281, died 1297
John de Taneto,	elected 1298, resigned 1307
John de Whatlington,	elected 1308, died 1311
John de Nortburne,	elected 1311, resigned 1318
John de Pevense,	elected 1318, died 1324
Alan de Retlyng,	elected 1324, died 1350 *(of the Black Death)*
Robert de Bello,	elected 1351, died 1364
Hamo de Offynton,	elected 1364, died 1383
John Crane,	elected 1383
John Lydbury,	elected 1398, died 1404
William Merssh,	elected 1405, died 1417
Thomas de Ludlow,	elected 1417, resigned 1435

It was in this Abbot's time that the Sword of Battle Abbey was made. His initials can be seen on each side of the coat of arms embossed on its hilt.

William Waller,	elected 1435, died 1437
Richard Dertmouth,	elected 1437, last mentioned 1461

Richard Dertmouth, the Abbey and all its servants were pardoned in 1450 for supporting the Cade Rebellion

John Newton,	elected 1463, died 1490
Richard Tovy,	elected 1490, died 1503
William Westfield,	elected 1503, died 1508

Lawrence Champion,   elected 1508, died 1529

Possible further Abbot 1529-31 as "On the Thursday after the feast of St.Laurence in 1529, a proxy from the Prior of Brecknock[34] was present in the Chapter-House in Battle, to elect a new Abbot". This may not have been John Hamond as he was still Sacristan in 1531, but it is possible that he had retained these duties as well as the Abbacy as there were so few monks by this time.

John Hamond,   elected 1529 or 1531, pensioned off 1538

The final act of surrender of the Abbey was signed by the last Abbot and all his monks. The Abbey seal was applied in white wax to the front and the Abbot's seal in red wax to the reverse of this document. This was the final act of the Abbey. The various letters, documents and events associated with this are described in detail in the Appendix.

---

34 Brecknock was a cell of Battle Abbey

Chapter 3
The Church of Saint Mary the Virgin
1102? - 2011

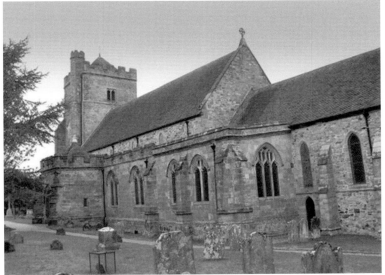

Figure 14. St Mary's Church from the south-east

Much has been written about Saint Mary's (Figs.14, B1 and B2) by local and other historians[35]. The objective of this book is to give a linking historic time-line overview of each church within the banlieu of Battle Abbey, so this chapter will focus as much as possible on the Church alone, only commenting in passing where this impinges on its former legal roles and roles in the local social governance of the parish, which have been well described elsewhere.

At first the Abbey would have shared its Church with the surrounding area, but as Battle grew larger the increasing numbers of people thronging the nave would have interfered with the Abbey's

---

35 Most recently in 2009 by Clifford Braybrooke in his self published book 'A History of the Parish Church of Battle'

religious purpose as a Benedictine Monastery.

The Abbey had had great economic success as a result of the expansion of agriculture in and around its banlieu and in its dealings with its extensive estate elsewhere in England and Wales. There was a need for markets and forges and tanneries and shoemakers and bakers and every other trade. The town of Battle grew and thrived to service the Abbey, finally obtaining its own momentum to grow even bigger.

The Abbey started building a chapel for the town sometime between 1102 and 1107. The monks in the inter-Abbacy and/or Abbot Ralph would have taken the active decision to provide the townsfolk with their own church building. The monks would have serviced the church at first but in 1115 a priest, Humphridus, was appointed by the Abbot to be their vicar. We even know where Humphridus lived which was the 89th messuage belonging to the Abbey estate, three properties to the east of St Mary's in the borough of Sandlake[36] (on the north side of the present Upper Lake). The priest was expected to pay seven pence per year for this dwelling and also provide at least one days labour.

From this point (1115) forwards, according to the Chronicles of Battle Abbey, the chaplain of St Mary's Church was a secular priest and not a monk. Hammond's interpretation of the Chronicle of Battle Abbey is that the monks said that the appointed priest 'should be acquainted with the affairs of the monastery, as if he were one of the monks....Being the one who has to act as Dean.' This was because the incumbent was in charge of a secular court dealing with civil matters, but may also have acted as a neutral Dean of the ecclesiastical court in the Abbey. This may be an early reason the title

---

36 This is the true origin of 'Senlac' which if used to name the Battle of Hastings is a retrospective romantic neologism. The name Senlac clearly did not exist in 1066. The original town of Battle was divided along the line of the ridge (taking the Abbey as its centre point) into western (Claverham) and eastern (Sandlake/Santelache) boroughs. Later there would also be boroughs of Middleborough in the area of the High Street and Mountjoy on the northern spur of the sandstone ridge, with Claverham persisting north and north-west of these. The Manor of Marley was created post 1310 to manage the lands of Uckham, Sedlescombe, Bathurst and Whatlington east and north-east of the banlieu.

Dean arose for the rector of St Mary's.

Before the Reformation this church would have been a pictorial wonder to its congregation. Internally it was extensively painted, with characters from the bible, stories of saints' lives, dooms, processions of souls and of devils. From the evidence left today most of the paintings were done with great skill possibly under supervision from the Abbey.

The wall paintings were obscured with lime wash after Henry VIII's reformation and were not seen again until the 19th century. Sketches and watercolours by Mr W H Brooke exist to show what they were like in 1845 when they may have been discovered before the removal of a gallery.

Figure 15. A sketch of the Doom which was over the Chancel arch. It is unusual in that both the living and the dead each have a seated figure. Same figure in colour at Figure B18.

They were again covered with whitewash until 1867, when they were partially restored by E Ward RA. But after that they were physically damaged during an enthusiastic Victorian 'renovation'. There was complete loss of the paintings above and around the nave arch, which extended onto the south wall of the nave, when the nave arch wall failed during the restoration of 1868. E C Rouse did further new restoration work in 1976-78 on the remaining paintings. Digital copies of watercolours and photographs of both the figures in the clerestory window splays and of the wall paintings are shown in Fig. 22 and in the second set of colour illustrations (Figures B1-7, B10-16 and B18).

After the dissolution by Henry VIII the last Abbot of Battle Abbey, John Hammond, received a pension of 100 Marks per annum and lived on in Battle for a further eight years. He requested in his will that on his death he be buried beneath St Catherine's aisle (see below, he would probably have regarded at that time the small south chapel as of St. Catherine). He left in his will, to be preserved in the south chapel, *'my two chasubles and that belongeth to them, also a chalice and paten double gilded and a scutcheon of silver in the foot of it.'* These no longer exist in Battle.

A gallery at the west end of the nave was erected in 1666. Perhaps it was a project to celebrate the 600th anniversary of 1066. This stayed in place for 202 years and an organ, purchased in 1837, was situated here when seen by J Vidler in 1841, until the gallery was demolished in the major renovation of 1868. It can be seen in W H Brooke's watercolours of 1845 (Figures B10 to B16 and B18). The organ was moved in 1868 to near the south chapel and replaced in 1950 by an electronic organ. This too was replaced as in 1974 it was decided to buy the redundant organ from the Central Methodist Church in Hastings which was closing and this was refurbished and re-installed in St Mary's.

Interest in this church is understandable both because its history is so closely linked to that of the Abbey itself, but also because of its own intrinsic architecture and features. To this can be added the fact that the original Royal Peculiar status of the Abbey covered the Church as well (negotiations to secure this are reported in the Chronicle of Battle Abbey) and continued to apply to the Church after the dissolution.

The Dean of Battle's Peculiar remained the lowey, liberty, leuga or banlieu (these are all synonyms) of Battle Abbey. Until 1 January 1846 the *'Court of the Peculiar of the Exempt Jurisdiction of the Deanery of Battle'* dealt with marriage licences and received wills and administrations and approved probate within this area, rather than the Archdeaconry of Lewes as would have been the case otherwise.

This is another, later, reason that the incumbent of Battle is still styled the Dean of Battle.

The Church lies in the Diocese of Chichester and the question of authority over the parish/banlieu with the Bishops of Chichester is recorded in the previous chapter. This tussle started in the 11th century and finally came to an end in 1846, surprisingly not in 1538. Until 1846 the Bishop had to enter the church at Battle with the permission of the Dean. An facsimile example of such a written request dating from 1762 is given below (Fig.16).

After 1846 the deanery became part of the Archdeaconry of Lewes; after 1912 it was in the Archdeaconry of Hastings. It is now part of the Deanery of Battle and Bexhill, part of the Lewes and Hastings Archdeaconry.

> *Whereas I an Desirous for the Ease of some Parishes in the Eastern Part of my Diocese to hold a Confirmation in the Parish Church of Battle I do hereby declare that I do it not by Virtue of any Episcopal Authority which I claim or intend to Exercise there But by the consent of the Revd Thos Nairn Dean of Battle to whom that Exempt Jurisdiction is granted*
>
> *July 17th 1762   W. Chichester*

Figure 16. Request from Bishop of Chichester to hold a confirmation in St. Mary's (as per church leaflet)

Before going on to the description of The Church and its architectural history there is a slight mystery to solve. The chapels to each side of the nave will need to be described below as north and south chapels to avoid confusions. This is because it seems that their names have changed over the years.

After the Reformation it appears that the north chapel was named after St Katherine[37] and the smaller south chapel after St Mary or just called the small chapel. Since the minor restoration of 1845 the north chapel has been called The Lady Chapel and the smaller south one St. Catherine's chapel. It is possible that this is a reversion to the names before the reformation when all references in Church of England churches to the Virgin Mary such as statues of the Madonna

---

37 St.Katherine and St.Catherine both appear at various times at the whim of the scribe no doubt.

and Lady Chapels were abolished as being redolent of popery. To swap the names of chapels is certainly not unknown. At Rye for example, the parish church transposed its chapels of St Nicholas and St Claire in Victorian times.

The church fabric is described in great detail by John Allen on his Sussex Parish Churches (SPC) website[38] and also to a lesser extent in a booklet available from the church itself. The following is modified from the SPC site with permission. It can be seen that the church has undergone many physical changes and renovations down the years. (Fig.17) Much of what can be seen today is the result of an extensive and to modern eyes a controversial Victorian renovation in Dean Crake's time.

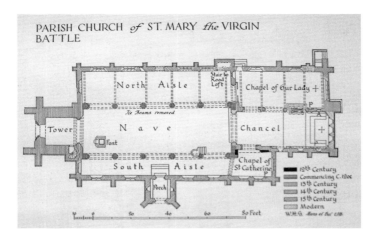

Figure 17. Historic plan by W.H.Godfrey of St Mary's from Victoria County History Vol.9

St. Mary's is a large church, lying across the road from the north battlement wall of Battle Abbey. It is originally 12th century, with an early 13th century nave. The chancel is a little later. The south aisle was remodelled in the 14th century and the north aisle in the 15th century, when the present west tower and two chapels were added. There are wall paintings of c.1300, fine monuments and brasses.

A large plain round-headed arch from the south chapel to the chancel is consistent with an early 12th century foundation. The wall around this is appreciably thicker, suggesting that there was a tower. If so, the first church was ambitious, with either a cruciform plan or a tower to one side of the chancel. What looks like a buttress at the south west corner of the north chapel may be a further 12th century remnant.

Figure 18. Internal view of western end of nave, southern aisle, west tower and door with the font central

The five-bay arcades show that the nave was started about 1200 and it may have had no predecessor. The chamfers on the pointed heads are slight and the piers are alternately round and square – the arcades are not symmetrical, with round piers opposite square ones. The capitals have varied foliage carving, except the moulded ones on both westernmost piers and the south west respond, which also have higher bases. They show that, as usual, the western bay was built last. The work is related to the arcade of similar date at Herstmonceux.

The eastern end was affected by the 19th century rebuilding of the chancel arch. This is like the arcades and, though wider than before, may incorporate early 13th century stones. The original head had alternating light and dark stones, a characteristic of around 1200.

There is doubt about the west end, particularly whether there was a tower here in the 13th century. If so, this implies any earlier one had gone. The reason for assuming that the lower part of the present tower is 13th century is the west doorway, which has three moulded orders on shafts (renewed). Everything else in the tower is 15th century and more probably the doorway was reset from the original west end.

The aisles have been rebuilt, but the relatively narrow south aisle has a lean-to roof and some of the footings of its eastern part and of the otherwise later porch are of rubble, suggesting its dimensions are 13th century. The present north aisle is broader and the west wall shows the line of the 13th century sloping roof and a trefoil lancet inside, by the arch from north chapel to aisle which originally opened onto the outside.

The upper parts of the nave have been altered; almost all the plain lancets of the clerestory are renewed and though the main timbers of the roof are 13th century and made, unusually, of chestnut wood, 19th century iron ties replace the wooden tie beams which are seen in pre-restoration drawings.

The nave was complete by 1230. Soon after, the chancel was rebuilt, almost certainly to be longer than before. Like the earlier 13th century work, it is built of rubble, with three south lancets, their sills connected outside by a string-course, interrupted by a doorway. Inside, only one shafted and roll-moulded wall-arch on the north side is intact. They are more complete to the south, with a stone seat along the base and a change in level in the second bay. The others to the north were replaced by arches to the chapel, when it was extended to the east. The three arches are mostly 14th century, but the complex moulded capitals and roll-moulded outer order on shafts of the westernmost are 13th century, so a chapel was intended from the outset.

A shaft on the chancel side is probably also 13th century, but not necessarily evidence of an intended vault. The east end has been twice altered, but the pinnacles at the angles were probably there from the start.

In the 14th century the south aisle was rebuilt in ashlar with battlements, though as already noted, probably on 13th century foundations. The mostly renewed pointed heads of the windows, with quatrefoils, are typical. The lower porch walls look 14th century, like the moulded archway and small square side-openings. The pyramid roof is not old, for Adelaide Tracy shows a flat one; there was probably an upper chamber, as at Rotherfield or Mayfield. The doorway is probably 14th century, but is repaired in cement. The north chapel was enlarged, with windows of reticulated tracery (renewed). The arches into the chancel are conventional 14th century except for the 13th century work already noted; the arch to the aisle is similar.

The chapel is stated by Meads to have a vaulted crypt, which he believed to have been inserted later. Boys-Behren records that a vault was constructed under the chancel by the will of Sir Whistler Webster in 1780. Whilst doing so the workmen discovered a small vault under the Brownes' tomb with three skeletons encased in lead, a male and female and a child. The sealed entry to the Webster crypt is obscured by a 1868 boiler room. Braybrooke discusses this and other ideas about the crypt in some detail.

The most obvious 15th century addition was the west tower, whether or not there was one before. Built of ashlar, it has angle-buttresses, an octagonal south east stair turret, square-headed bell-openings and battlements around a low tiled pyramid. The tower contained eight bells in 1841 as described by J. Vidler (writing as 'The Gleaner'), but at least some of these must have been replaced as the bells at present date from between 1803 and 1890. In 2011 structural repairs were necessary to the medieval roof and beams in the tower and the whole tower was re-pointed. The bells are rung every Sunday and the bell-ringers practice very Tuesday evening. For campanologists the details of the present bells are listed below. Four appear to have been replaced since J Vidler's time (1841) and there is a record of the bells having been possibly rung as a peal in 1739 by a visiting team of bell-ringers from Wye in Kent, but no details can be found of the bells' history before that. As can be seen the largest bell weighs over one tonne.

Bell No.	cwt	qtr	lbs	kg	Tone	Date	Founder
1	5	2	5	282	E flat	1869	Robert Stainbank
2	6	0	24	316	D	1815	Thomas II Mears
3	6	1	18	326	C	1874	Mears & Stainbank
4	7	2	18	389	B flat	1803	Thomas I Mears
5	9	1	17	478	A flat	1803	Thomas I Mears
6	10	3	18	554	G	1869	Mears & Stainbank
7	14	2	0	737	F	1890	John Warner & Sons
8	21	3	8	1109	E flat	1825	Thomas II Mears

The tower arch has two continuous orders and an inner one on semi-octagonal responds. The four-light west window has panelled tracery. An angled lancet-like opening above the moulded north doorway (now concealed), noted by Hussey, can hardly have been a squint for an anchorite (a religious recluse) in view of its position. It has been suggested that it was a simple vent for candle smoke.

The north aisle was widened with a gable and three-light windows like the west one of the tower. It is built of rubble, possibly because the north side was less conspicuous. Outside, a rood-stair projects near the east end; only the blocked lower entrance remains inside. The position of the stair indicates that the loft extended across nave and aisles. Hussey records openings by the chancel arch and to the north aisle which confirm such an arrangement.

The smaller south chapel, also 15th century, has a plain parapet and panelled tracery. If the tower stood here until the present west one was built, the chapel may date from after its removal. A smaller pointed arch with semi-octagonal responds was inserted in the 12th century one to the chancel. A double-chamfered half-arch into the south aisle is angled to support the east wall of the nave. Its outer respond has a semi-octagonal shaft. Of the niches in the south and east walls, those by the east window, though damaged, have vaulted heads. The presumed lancets of the main east window were replaced by five lights of panelled tracery, as Quartermain shows, but changes make certainty impossible.

The adjacent pinnacles, probably 13th century in origin, seem to have been altered. The only obvious later change on the Sharpe Collection drawing of c.1797 is the south porch roof. There were new pews in 1839 and a minor restoration in 1845-46 , when the wall-paintings were discovered and fortunately copied.

In 1867-69 W Butterfield restored the whole church except the tower. He was aiming for a Victorian Gothic appearance. He removed the gallery which had been there for 202 years. He replaced most external stonework, with little change except at the east end, where the 15th century window gave way to three stepped lancets in a single arch. He may also have altered the pinnacles to give them what he considered a more 13th century form. All the roofs are his except for the nave, where he inserted iron ties to replace the wooden tie beams.

To improve the sight lines, he recommended widening the chancel arch. This was on the 'wish list' of the church, if it could be afforded, but Butterfield seemed determined to include this if at all possible. From his point of view it was a bonus that the nave arch wall threatened to collapse, possibly secondarily to the removal of the tie beams and had to be demolished. This caused the loss of the all the wall paintings on the walls around and above the nave arch, which is indeed larger than before and now noticeably off-centre. It is now aligned with the chancel whereas previously it was symmetrical with the nave. A line drawing of the nave before Butterfield's restoration and a comparison with a photograph of the same view today are shown in Figs. 20 and 21. The prior wooden tie beams are replaced by steel rods, the nave arch is off centre to the nave (but not the chancel) and there is complete loss of the wall paintings of the Chancel arch wall and on the south wall. The paintings on the north wall are all damaged to some extent.

Dean Youell commented in his booklet on the church – 'It is difficult to forgive Butterfield for denuding the roof of the ancient tie beams and king-posts', although he did understand that some work on the nave arch was needed as the 'wall was falling down'.

The final bill for the restoration was £4736 2s 1d, a huge amount at that time and further work to the tower and to the church clock had to be postponed. This and further work took place at one or more later dates.

The tower has been restored, but the shafted rere-arch of Butterfield's east window is apparently not to his plan. In the 20th century a vestry was added to the north aisle, concealing a 15th century doorway. The only name recorded is P A Robson, said to have done unspecified work before 1914 . A new extension with meeting rooms and other facilities is being added in 2011 with access via the vestry door.

Fittings and monuments

Aumbry (cabinet for chalices etc.): (Under north lancet of chancel) 13th century, large and square.

Font: Late 12th century Purbeck marble. The largest of the type with square arcaded marble bowl, common in Sussex. It stands on a centre-stem and four renewed corner-shafts.

Font cover: 15th century, though much restored. It is octagonal and domed with a large finial.

Brasses (Sketches Fig. 19):

1. John Low (d1426). Worn and wearing full armour. (North chapel)
2. William Arnold (d1435) Small armoured half-figure. Both this and that to John Low are given to the quantitatively small Series E (see London workshops). (Concealed)
3. Robert Clare (d1450), Dean, vested for mass, with a hound at his feet. This also appears to belong to Series E, though most authorities assign it to a rather earlier date. However, the date of c1430 appears too early, as Clare only became Dean in 1440 and the inscription refers to him as this (Sanctuary)
4. Thomas (d1589) and Elizabeth (d1590) Alfraye. Only the female figure is left. (East end of north aisle)
5. John Wythines (d1615), Dean, shown in contemporary academic dress. (Sanctuary)

Figure 19. Copies of the brasses

Dean Robert Clere
1440

William Arnold Esq.
Dec. 29. 1435

John Lowe
Nov. 15. 1426

Elizabeth Comfort
1501

John Wythines D.D.
May 18. 1615

Glass:
(North aisle) C15 fragments in two windows,   including a complete bust of a bishop. A figure of St Catherine mentioned by Horsfield is not to be seen.
(West window) A Gibbs, 1882 (four prophets)
(East window) Burlison and Grylls, 1900
(South chancel, third window) J Powell and Son, 1885
(South aisle, first window) M C F Bell, 1984 (signed).
(North chapel, second window) J Powell and Son, designed by H Holiday (Fig. B8)
The Senlac Window, M C F Bell, 1984 (see second set of colour illustrations Fig. B9)

Figures 20 (above) and 21 (below). Comparison views of the nave and chancel arch before the major restoration of Butterfield (sketch) and today (photograph). Note the extent of the wall paintings over the chancel arch, extending onto the south nave wall. These were destroyed and those on the north nave wall were all damaged to a greater or lesser degree. Also note the new larger offset chancel arch and the changes to the chancel east window.

Monuments:

(Easternmost arch from chancel to north chapel)Tomb of   Sir Anthony Browne (d.1548) and his first wife Alys (Figure B17). He acquired the abbey after the Dissolution and the tomb combines old and new ideas. The alabaster effigies are of different lengths, so his wife has a canopy. He is shown in armour and both are praying, though the hands are lost. This is fairly traditional, but the chest is Renaissance in design, divided into three parts by balusters. Each has an arched top in the form of a shell and contains a cherub with outstretched wings. Beneath is a shield in a wreath with more cherubs as supporters. The monument has been repainted fairly recently. See colour insert.

(Churchyard near east end) Tombstone of Isaac Ingall (d1798). Said to have been 120 years old and to have been butler at the Abbey for 95 years.

(West end of the north wall of the nave) The Cartwright Memorial. The inventor of the power loom the Rev. Dr. Edmund Cartwright, DD FRS was originally born in Marham, Norfolk in 1743. He obtained patents on the design of power looms in 1785 and 1787, but resistance to their introduction caused him to be bankrupted in 1793. His patents expired but he was eventually awarded £10,000 by Parliament which enabled him to retire, to Hollenden in Kent at the age of seventy. He died in 1823 whilst in Hastings on a fashionable sea-bathing visit and was fortuitously buried at Battle as the then Dean was a close friend.

Dating from before 1900 there are a number of memorials to valued local people who fell in war, but only after 1900 are the common people remembered. There are two memorials to the fallen of the Boer War plus a memorial to members of the congregation who died in WW2. The Battle War Memorial stands in the churchyard, a gift of Dean Currie and his wife in 1920.

Wall Paintings: (Above north arcade) These were found in 1845, but re-covered with whitewash until 1867, when they were partially restored by E Ward RA. E C Rouse did further work in 1976-78. The main series, between the clerestory windows on the north side, of c.1300 shows the life of St. Margaret of Antioch in two tiers, each scene in a frame. The series starts at the right hand (east) end with the upper row and reads leftwards to the end, then down to the lower row when the scenes return rightwards. They show in order 1-24 the birth of the Saint, her being handed over to her Christian nurse, the approach of the Roman Provost Olybrius and her subsequent tortures, finally her execution, burial, and her soul being received into Heaven (Figs. 22 and B4 to B7).

In the splays of the clerestory windows are large figures, though only Moses in the westernmost opening can be identified for sure. Though faded, the colour and drawing suggest a skilled master, possibly linked with the abbey (Figs. B3, B10 and B11).

To the right of the easternmost northern clerestory window, partially hidden behind the organ is the start of a scene of a great procession of Blessed Souls about to be received into heaven by St. Peter, part of the Last Judgement (Fig.B14). This is obscured but is the first part of a long wall painting which extended right across the nave wall to be reflected on the opposite wall, finishing left of the easternmost south wall clerestory window. At this point St. Peter is seen seated in front of the Gates of Heaven with souls kneeling before him (Fig. B15).

Over the chancel arch, above the procession, was a Doom (Figs. 15 and B18), with three living and three dead, slightly unusual in that one of each set of characters is sitting.

An album of W H Brooke's watercolours, commissioned by W H Beresford-Hope of Bedgebury Park is now held at ESRO[39] . An interpretation by E C Rouse of the watercolours of the lost wall paintings, is repeated in Vere Hodge's booklet. Rouse provisionally dated them as between the 13th and early 14th century in origin, with the window splay figures possibly being 16th century. It is a great shame that some of the originals have been lost forever.

A selection are copied, together with other views of the church in the colour illustrations, Figs.B10-B16 plus B18).

Piscinae (stone basins):

1. (Chancel south east bay) Complex 13th century, with three trefoils above a cusped head.

2. (South chapel) 15th century trefoil-headed. Damaged.

3. (North chapel) 14th century ogee-cinquefoiled double one.

Pulpit: 1869, designed by Butterfield, with foliage carved by T Earp

Reredos: (and altar) 1929, by C J Blomfield

Figure 22. **The two middle sets of north wall paintings, between clerestory windows. Upper parts and some other sections of the paintings have been obliterated - but see the colour inserts for more photographic detail (Figs. B3-B7)**

Parish Priests/Deans

Presumably from its foundation to the appointment of the first priest the church was served directly by monks from the Abbey.

Several sources exist for the list below:
These are: The board in the Church : The list given by Lilian Boys-Behren which she would have almost certainly obtained via the Duchess of Cleveland's publications : The list of Dean Youard made sometime between 1924-1946 : Chronicle of Battle Abbey : The Clergy of the Church of England on-line database : Harleian MS. 3586 (as per Boys-Behren and Youard): Thorpe's Descriptive

Catalogue : Papal Regesta 231 fo.60 (1355).

Additions/changes to the Church board data are given in **bold font**.
Information about the earliest years including the reluctance of John
(1175) to take the post and move to Battle and the appointment of
Walter come from the Chronicle of Battle Abbey. The date of
appointment of Humphry (Humphridus) is unclear. The first part of
the Chronicle was written circa. 1155 and he is recorded as living in
one of the Abbey's messuages at that time.

Humphridus	**bef. 1155 d.1171**

*The Chronicle of Battle Abbey records difficulties recruiting a priest after
the death of Humphrey and the church was again served by monks from the
Abbey.*

(John)	1175

*John never took up the post, he wished to hold it 'in absentia' and this was
never accepted*

Walter	1176 - ?

*It is highly unlikely that Walter served for 70 years. Again the monks may
have served or the next incumbent may have taken over sooner rather than
later.*

Magister A de R	**? - 1246**

*'Magister' is Latin for 'Master' and the the three entries with this form
come from the Harleian MS.3586.*

Magister C de D	**1246 - 1250**
Richard	1250 - 1277
John de Wygepain	1277 - **1305**
Magister R de L	**1305 - 1330**
John de Wyperitye	**1331 – 1349**

*It has been conjectured that the two J de Ws were the same person. If so he
would have ministered for 72 years, again highly unlikely - and how would
Mag. R de L have fitted in? It may be the J de Ws are related but not the
same person.*

Figure B1. St Mary's Church from the Abbey battlements

Figure B2. St Mary's interior from the west door

Figures B3a-B3f. Figures in the splays of three of the north clerestory windows in St Mary's Church Looking north - west to east: 1st two images westernmost window splay window paintings, no paintings on second splays, 2nd two images in third splays, final two images paintings in easternmost spalys. The 1st painting is believed to be Moses. The others are not clearly identified although John Allen has suggested the last may be St. Christopher.

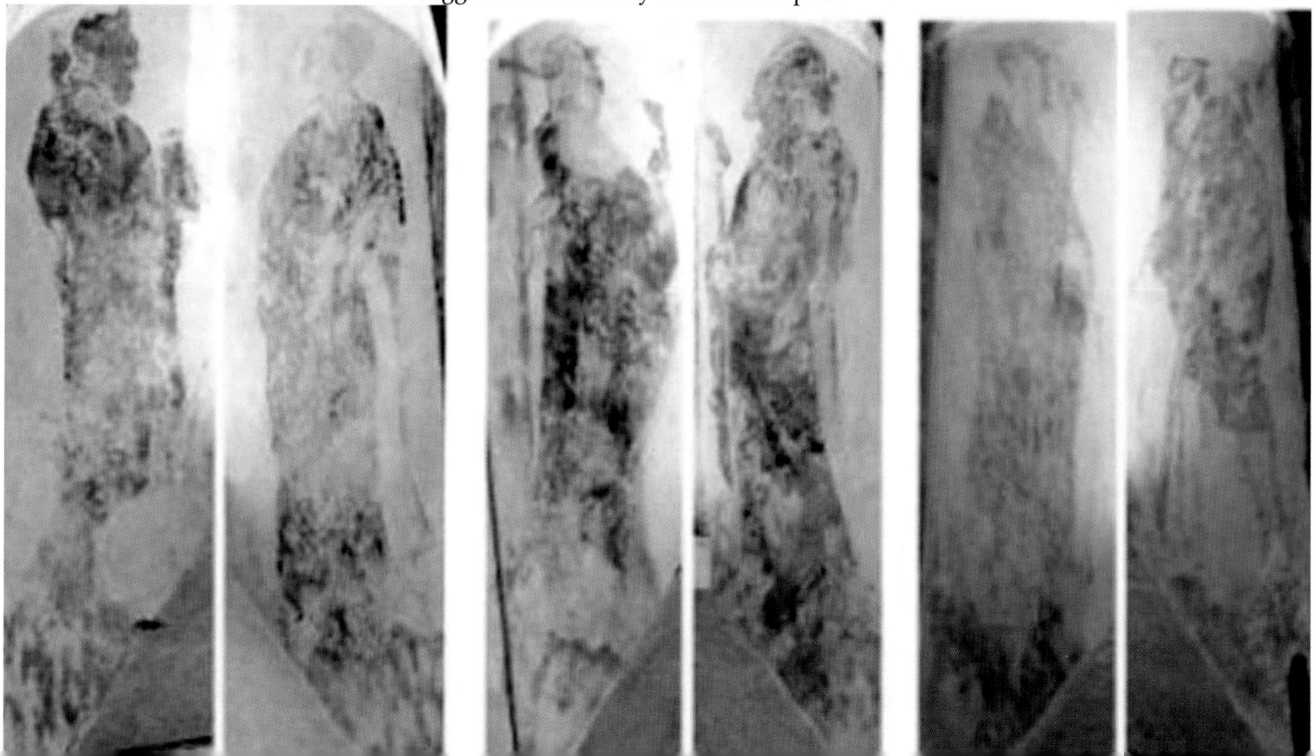

Figure B4. First and last sets (eastern end) Pictures of the life of St Margaret of Antioch. There are 24 panels in all which need to be read right to left on the top row, then left to right on the bottom row (as numbered). They were significantly damaged during a major restoration

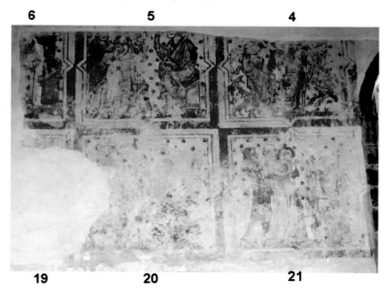

Figure B5 Second and seventh sets (second from east end)

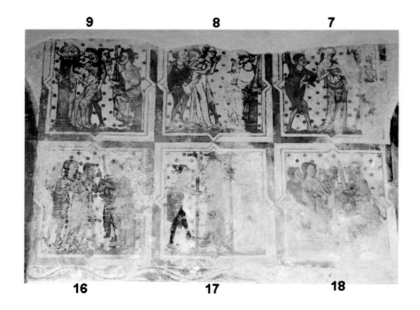

Figure B6 Third and sixth sets (second from west end)

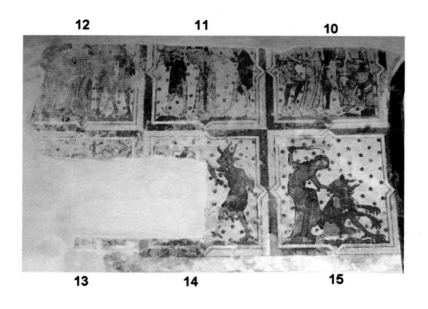

Figure B7. Fourth and fifth sets (westernmost end)

Figure B8. The east window in the Chapel of Our Lady, St Mary's Parish Church

Figure B9. The Senlac Window

W H Brooke's watercolours

Figures B10 and B11 above: West clerestory window splay paintings

Figure B12 below. Old gallery and the western most wall paintings.

If the colours are recorded faithfully comparison with 2011 photographs shows that there must have been considerable fading and deterioration since this recording.

Figure B13. The box pews and gallery plus the second set of wall paintings. This also shows the now missing 2nd from west window splay figures .

Figure B14. The east end of the north nave wall.
Now obscured by the organ, the start of the procession of souls to the gates
of heaven (lower row of wall paintings).
This procession extended across the chancel arch wall to be reflected onto
the south nave wall.

Figure B15. The eastern end of the south nave wall.
The end of the procession as before and above this St Peter at the gates of
Heaven.
All destroyed during the renovation.

Figure B16. The inside of the St Mary's church viewed from the west door looking east.

Note the box pews, wall paintings, small chancel arch centred to the nave, the old pulpit and tie beams. The font cover is plain, not red as at present.

Figure B17. Tomb of Sir Anthony Browne and his first wife Alys

Figure B18. Watercolour sketch of the Doom

Watercolours all © East Sussex Record Office

Photographs by the author

Geoffrey de Ludeford	1350
John de Kele	1350-1
Simon de Brantyngham	1350-1
William de Ludbury	?

This was time of plague in Battle. The population of the town fell 50% and 30% of the monks died including the Abbot. Perhaps for this reason the new Abbot (Robert de Bello) failed to fill the vacancy for several years. Eventually the Pope instructed the Dean of London to appoint John de Torkesey in 1355[40]

John de Torkesey	1355 - 1375
William Baroun	1375 (for four months only)
William (G)Jutherlane	1376 - 1389
John Wotton	1389 - 1390
Thomas Talbot	1390 - 1396
Hamo Offyngton	1397[41]- 1406
Nicholas Balle	1406 - 1415
Thomas Rok(e)	1416 - 1433
John Farleigh	1433 - 1439
Robert Maslyn	1439 - 1440
Robert Clere	1440 – 1450 (brass in church)
Robert Alleyn	**1450 - 1485**
Robert Selrugh/Sebourgh	1486 - ?
William Mille	? - 1501
John Oxenbridge	1501 – circa. 1528
William (Y)Inold	**circa. 1528** - 1545
Elizeus Ambrose	1545 - 1572
John Wythines	**1572** – 1615 (brass in church)
Thomas Bambridge	1615 - 1628
Christopher Dowe	1629 - 1632
Robert Acre	1633 - 1642

---

40 4 Kal. Nov. Avignon. (f. 60.) To the dean of London, the archdeacon of
     Colchester, and another named. Mandate to induct John de Torkesey, B.C.L.
     into the deanery of Battle, value 20 marks, void by the death of William de
     Ludbury, so long ago that it has lapsed to the pope, notwithstanding that he
     has papal provision of the chaplaincy of Stanford, in the diocese of London.
41 Nephew of the Abbot of Battle of the same name

No signature on churchwardens accounts 1643-4. The Civil Wars started in 1642.

Henry Fisher   **circa.1645 – 1664**

Henry Fisher has been recorded elsewhere as Oliver Cromwell's chaplain although the author has not been able to confirm this and others are so designated. It may be that he was a chaplain in the New Model Army and as such would have been a Presbyterian. If so unless he signed the Act of Uniformity in 1662 his position would have been precarious.

Dr. William Watson	1664 - 1689
Dr. William Simmons	1689 - 1730
Richard Nairne	1731 - 1760
Thomas Nairne	1760 - 1776
John(s(t)on) Lawson	1776 - 1779
Dr. Thomas Ferris	1779 - 1801
Dr. Thomas Birch	1801 – 1836

also Archdeacon of Lewes from 1823

John Littler	1836 -1863
Dr. Edward N Crake	1863 – 1882

founder of the Church of the Ascension, Telham

Dr. Edward R Currie	1882 - 1920
Henry Francis	1920 - 1924
Wilfrid Youard	1924 - 1946
Arthur Naylor DSO, OBE	1946 – 1960

Hon. Chaplain to King George VI

Francis Outram	1960 - 1970
Richard Darby	1970 – 1975

first Dean to preach in the Baptist Church

Rex Bird	1975 - 1984
John Chater	1984 – 1991
William Cummings	1991 - 2005
Dr. John Edmondson	2005 -

Chapter 4
Times of Change 1531 – 1858

In 1531 King Henry VIII declared himself to be supreme head of the Church of England. After this the royal coat of arms was hung in churches to symbolise this, although they were briefly removed during the short reign of Queen Mary I and during the Commonwealth when the monarchy was abolished.

This pronunciation was legitimised by two Acts of Parliament in 1532 and 1534, which declared Henry VIII and his successors head of the Church in England and gave the Crown straight away one year's income of every church, cathedral and monastery, to be followed by 10% of their incomes per annum (this would previously have gone to the Pope).

Obviously Henry VIII wanted to know just how much he was getting and he set up a survey – the *Valor Ecclesiasticus temp Henry VIII*. Having learnt the value of the monasteries Henry then decided to plunder them. The Dissolution of the Monasteries began in 1536 and by 1540 all the monasteries of England and Wales were closed.

The obvious effect of this on Battle was two fold. Firstly the Abbey Church was razed and its belongings if valuable were given to the crown or kept by the new lord of the manor, Sir Anthony Browne, who was secondly only interested in making money out of his new estates. So the relationship between the Abbey manor and the local inhabitants changed from one of essentially mutual benefit to that of lord and servants. The services many locals did for the abbey were sometimes no longer required and the hereditary leasehold tenancies became vulnerable, although it seems no immediate changes were made.

When Henry VIII died in 1547 his son Edward VI (1547-53) succeeded and the Church of England became more obviously Protestant. The changes were great and included the destruction of images - so wall-paintings were lime-washed over and statues and rood-screens removed. Lady Chapels, with their references to the

Virgin Mary, emblematic of Catholicism, were either removed or converted to other use.

The simple Protestant liturgy also made many church objects redundant, so the Crown promptly confiscated these church goods too in 1552. This generated inventories of plate for every church. These inventories can be seen to this day in the National Archives.

So Battle Parish Church changed. Its extensive medieval wall paintings were lime-washed over, not to be seen again for nearly 300 years. Anything to do with Catholicism was removed. Its valuables ended up in Henry's coffers.

The vicar or dean until now had been a Catholic priest and this too changed with the appointment of a Protestant Church of England Dean under the patronage (advowson) of the new secular lord of the manor.

On the plus side a new house (Fig. 23) was built soon after 1538 for the new incumbent and this fine Elizabethan Deanery, which is now in private ownership, stands behind and below the church. The Dean now lives in a modern deanery on Caldbec Hill. The old deanery was built soon after 1538 of red brick with stone quoins for the incumbent of the church, but a Dean's flower garden is recorded in 1304 and there were presumably earlier buildings on this site.

As has been previously noted the former priest's house was three houses away from the church on the south side of Upper Lake.

In 1669 Dr William Watson added stables and re-arranged the interior in 1677 and in about 1863 Dr Edward Neville Crake made alterations to the rear and built a porch. There are two lead rainwater pipe heads with the initials WW, a fleur de lys and the date 1669.

Edward VI was not strong in health and may well have suffered from congenital syphilis. When he died young his older half-sister Mary I became Queen. She promptly restored Catholicism in 1555 amid much unpleasantness and martyrdom of Protestants, but she too had a short reign, dying of what is believed to have been ovarian cancer. Sir Anthony Browne's son, also Anthony, lord of the manor of Battle, was active in her service and was made Lord Montagu.

There still being no male heir, the last child of Henry VIII, Elizabeth I, daughter of the ill fated and beheaded Ann Boleyn, became Queen. She promptly reversed the Acts of Mary in 1559 and restored

Protestant uniformity to religious services.

Figure 23. The Elizabethan Deanery

It is unlikely that any major changes occurred in Battle in the Marian period between 1555 and 1559 apart from the temporary removal of the royal crest from the building. The Dean must have not quite known what to do at this confusing juncture.

Catholics continued to have a very difficult time after 1559 and in 1593 an Act of Parliament was passed providing for the imprisonment of those attending a Roman Catholic service.

On Elizabeth I's death the crown passed to the Stuart dynasty. England and Scotland were united - which in religious terms was interesting - as Presbyterianism was the national Church of Scotland. In short, this led to further religious confusions. James I and Charles I continuously quarrelled with their Parliaments.

James I was sillier than Elizabeth. He had grandiose theories of the divine right of kings and there was a growing tension and divergence between King and Parliament. Two social systems and their ideologies were in conflict. Presbyterianism, which had its origins in Scotland, advocated abolition of the royally appointed bishops and removal of the domination of local Churches by local landowners and gentry. This was an oligarchical theory which appealed greatly to the growing English merchant classes represented in the Parliament and by 1640 most classes were united against the King.

This led inevitably to the Civil War from 1642 which pitted supporters of Parliament against the Crown, the trial and execution of Charles I on 30 January 1649, the replacement of the monarchy with the Commonwealth republic which ruled first England, and then Ireland and Scotland from 1649 to 1660 and established Presbyterianism as the State Church in England as well as in Scotland.

The ultimate outcome of the Revolution was the dumping of the idea of the divine right of kings, the realisation of the fact that parliament was supreme in political matters, and that the English monarch had to be a constitutional monarch. The monarchy was restored on these terms in 1660, although it was not until the Glorious Revolution 28 years later that this was fully legitimised.

The breakdown of religious uniformity and the incomplete Presbyterian Settlement of 1646 (i.e. the half-Puritanisation of the Church of England) enabled independent churches to flourish. Although most Presbyterians welcomed the Restoration in 1660, the Puritan reforms of the Church of England were quickly revoked under the restored Stuart regime. Under the Act of Uniformity (May 1662), all English clergymen had to pass three tests or lose their livings. They had to use the revised Book of Common Prayer, renounce the Solemn League and Covenant (one of whose objectives had been to unite the Churches of Scotland and England under a Presbyterian system of church government) and be ordained by a bishop. It is estimated that 2000 Presbyterian and non-conformist clergymen were ejected from their livings on St. Bartholomew's Day (24 August) 1662 for refusing to comply. They must have been bitter having previously welcomed the Restoration – it was a lesson into the perils of religious politics.

Later, there was fear that James II, who foolishly and obviously had not studied his history well enough, would try to re-establish Catholicism. This led to the Glorious Revolution of 1688. James was deposed in favour of his daughter Mary who was married to the

Protestant William of Orange and they reigned as joint sovereigns, William III and Mary II. This was the time at which the full supremacy of Parliament was finalised.

An Act of Toleration was passed in 1689, which permitted freedom of worship to Protestant dissenters (though it still excluded Roman Catholics.)

This Act required the registration of dissenters' meeting houses. It is from the records of this registration that we find diverse Non-conformist groups registered in Battle in the 19th century

It took another 100 years until 1791 for the Roman Catholic Relief Act to allow Catholics to worship in churches with unlocked doors. This act also required the registration of Roman Catholic churches in England and Wales.

From its earliest days Christianity has always had its dissenters. For most of its history, the established Church in England be it Catholic or Conformist or Non-conformist Protestant, has condemned those deviating from the perceived norm and punished them with varying degrees of severity and sometimes downright barbarity. The establishment of the Church of England at the Reformation of Henry VIII had simply changed the head of the Church from the Pope to the Crown. Unfortunately it did not herald a new era of general tolerance. Despite more central government toleration extreme sects were still opposed by the upper and propertied classes as they were seen as a threat to social order and property rights.

The word Non-conformist was originally used for anyone who refused to conform to the Act of Uniformity of 1662. The term was later applied to a wide variety of sects with one thing in common - their difference from the established Church, as long as they were not Catholics.

Early Non-conformist chapels tended to be plain, rectangular structures and many chapels continued in that style into the 19th century. Some preferred two-storey chapels with a classical façade and an internal gallery on the upper storey. In Battle the Zion Baptist and Methodist Churches (Figs. 34 and 43) and the closed and demolished Unitarian chapel all conformed to this model, indeed the Unitarian chapel may have had two galleries. The old Methodist chapel lost its small gallery when it was removed in 1990, when it was feared it would collapse. The gallery in the Zion Chapel still exists.

The rise in population in 19th-century England generated an explosion of church-building, Conformist and Non-conformist. Anxious to counter the rise of dissent the government allocated £1M in 1818 towards Church of England church building. By 1858 over 3,000 new churches had been built. This as a side effect started the education of the masses as many church schools sprang up alongside these new foundations.

Locally Netherfield church and the Church of the Ascension at Telham were built in this period or soon afterwards, although the financing of the latter was unusual as we shall see later.

Chapter 5
Presbyterians from 1696-1773 - then Independent Calvinists 1776 – 1780 - then the Baptist Calvinist Church of God 1780 – 1793

In England Presbyterianism was established in secret in 1572. Thomas Cartwright is thought to have been the first English Presbyterian and his controversial lectures at Cambridge University condemning the hierarchy of the Elizabethan Church of England led to his dismissal by Archbishop John Whitgift and his prudent emigration abroad.

During the Commonwealth England and Wales followed Scotland in turning to Presbyterianism. In 1643 Parliament abolished diocesan administration and in 1646 the offices of archbishop and bishop were formally abolished. In 1647, by an act of the Long Parliament under the control of Puritans, the Church of England permitted Presbyterianism. However, the situation concerning dioceses was reversed at the Restoration in 1660, so the break in diocesan records was comparatively short. The re-establishment of the monarchy in 1660 brought the return of Episcopal church government in England, but the Presbyterian church in England continued in non-conformity outside of the established church. The ministers displaced under the Act of Uniformity (1662) had a very difficult time until in 1672 they could become licensed to hold services.

In 1696 the Rev. Burnard[42], a Presbyterian disciple, settled at Lewes. Soon afterwards he started undertaking regular visits to Battle, nearly 40 km (24 miles) away. He probably did a circuit of villages and towns but Burnard's zeal must have been very great because

---

42 This must refer to T homas Barnard b.1643 (in Lewes) who became joint pastor with the Rev Edward Newton at a private house in Lewes in August 1695. He was the son of a prosperous Lewes draper who also had a farm at Northease. He ministered from 1673, but was not ordained until 1687 at Glyndebourne. His wider ministry does appear to have been active from before 1696 as there is a record that he baptised someone in the sea near Hastings in 1691.

travelling around Sussex in those days was not easy. The result of his endeavours was the establishment in Battle in 1716 of a resident Presbyterian minister, a Mr. William Potter, a "gentleman of character and ability."

Following this the Presbyterians led the way for non-conformity in Battle, forming a congregation of some size (120 persons in 1717, out of a possible population of approx.600)[43] [44]and owning a building on Mount Street for their meetings. The second Battle Presbyterian minister was the Rev. Samuel Ashmore, followed by the Rev. John Smith. He in turn was succeeded in 1740 by the Rev. John Whittel, who moved to Brighton in about 1747, when the Rev. David Jenkins took over.

At the beginning of the Rev. Jenkins' twenty-five years the Presbyterians were flourishing and he was said to have been "evangelical and able". As years went on he apparently found it increasingly difficult to cope with the Universalist doctrine that was spreading and Presbyterianism petered out in Battle by 1773. For some years the chapel was closed and the residual congregation must have worshipped in members' houses.

Just after the death of David Jenkins, George Gilbert, an Independent Calvinist from Heathfield, known as the "Apostle of Sussex," came to Battle to hold services. *"The occasion of Mr. Gilbert's coming to the town,"* says William Vidler (who will himself be a critical person in 1793) *"was thus: There was a poor man, one William Sweetenham, that came from Brighton to Battle to make bricks. This person loved the Gospel, but he could go nowhere to hear it nearer than Heathfield, which is ten miles from Battle; he therefore gave Mr. Gilbert an invitation to come to his house to preach. He accepted the invitation and in January, 1776, he came and preached to about 40 people in the evening, and the Word seemed to be well received."*

George Gilbert paid further visits in February and March, after which Mr. Sweetenham's landlord forbade the preaching

---

43 The population had been static for a while but grew quite rapidly after this to 2040 by 1801 and 3039 by 1841

44 This was an unusually large proportion of the local population, the only place in Sussex with a larger Nonconformist population was Rye with 50% of the familes being Nonconformists.

(presumably it was loud) and a "conversation" took place instead. *"Several persons seemed to be in earnest about their salvation, the appearance of which set the whole town in confusion."* The Battle group also had visits from preachers supported by the Countess of Huntingdon[45] who gave money to support the Calvinist Methodist cause including support for the building of 64 chapels.

George Gilbert was obviously a man of charisma. He was born at Rotherfield in 1741 and was said to have been "A wild, reckless and immoral soldier." In 1759 he had joined a regiment of light horse under General Elliott, who was engaged in defending Hanoverian interests against the French. He went through three campaigns of the "Seven Years' War" and distinguished himself by capturing a French standard; so he was a brave man as well. He returned to England in 1763. Soon after, while at Nottingham in 1766, Gilbert was converted to 'Methodism'. After this he became an overseer on the estate of his former commanding officer, by now Lord Heathfield, at Heathfield Park. Presumably by then he was no longer 'wild, reckless and immoral' and Lord Heathfield had recognised that.

He went around Sussex villages conducting religious meetings. He first concentrated on Rotherfield, then Crowborough. His spare time was filled with village preaching *"till he had introduced the message of His mercy into more than forty different parishes."* He eventually became pastor of an Independent chapel at Heathfield being paid £28 per year, later £40. He built his own house and filled it mainly with furniture that he made himself. He stepped down and became an an Assistant Minister in 1809 and died on 23rd March 1827, aged 86 years, after a ministry of 60 years.

Following Gilbert's visits when he preached under the Watch or Great Oak at the north entrance to the town, a small group of people formed an Independent Calvinist Church in Battle in 1776. They gathered regularly for worship, initially worshipping in a room of a

---

45 Selina Shirley, the daughter of Earl Ferrers, was born in 1707. When she was twenty-one she married the Earl of Huntingdon. She joined the Calvinistic Methodists in 1739 and nine years later made George Whitefield, her chaplain. Whitefield's followers became known as the the Countess of Huntingdon's Connexion.

house in The Mount[46]. A youth called William Vidler joined this church and the next year he started lay-preaching. Under Vidler's Independent ministry, while he still worked as a stonemason, the number of members rose rapidly from 15 to 150.

Figure 24. The Baptist Calvinist Chapel from a journal © ESRO

It seems that from 1777-1780 there was no formal minister, but in 1780 Vidler and some others, persuaded of the correctness of believer's baptism (as opposed to infant baptism), were baptised by Thomas Purdy, a Baptist minister in Rye. A majority of the Independent Calvinist Church then re-organised as a Baptist Calvinist Church on 28 March 1780. Nicholas and William Slatter, Joseph Fuller, Daniel Wood, Thomas Mepham, Edward French, William Ashby, Thomas and Ann Hasleden, Stephen Spilstead, Charity Sweetenham, and Elizabeth Ashdown were its first signed up members, with William Ashby elected Deacon, they then called William Vidler as minister. In addition there is a record of the appointment of J Parker as Deacon, 25 Dec 1780.

---

46   Mount Street

It is therefore from 28 March 1780 that the 'Baptist Calvinist Church of God' at Battle existed. At first they met in a house on 'The Mount' possibly the same house as mentioned above, but in 1782 this church bought a house described as 'the old Presbyterian building'. This may be the piece of land of 400 sq m (1/10th acre) with an 'edifice or building called a meeting place' described in a 99 year lease from Sir Godfrey Webster to Lester Harvey Esq., dated 5 April 1791 with a ground rent of one old penny per year[47]. Just who Lester Harvey was is not clear, but he may have acted as an intermediary and then re-assigned the lease to the Church. The Church members had pulled this old Meeting House down in 1789 and also bought just over 890 sq m (1/5th acre) of part of an adjacent orchard for £60. This left them £160 in debt for the land, most of which was found from members and friends. They then created a new church 13.4 m (44 feet) long and 9.75 m (32 feet) wide with two balconies and a vestry plus a burial ground (Figs.24 and 27). The new building opened on 11 April 1790, but left them with another debt of £700.

Consulting the tithe map of 1840 and the Ordnance Survey map of 1873 (Figs. C3 and C4), this chapel stood on the same side but further up Mount Street towards Caldbec Hill than today's Zion Chapel and was set back some distance from the road in its own churchyard. Mountjoy did not exist as a road at that time, but there was a footpath corresponding to it and this was the northern boundary of the site. The details of the changes in this area to the present day will be found in Chapter 14.

In the next two or three years chapel affairs became turbulent and Vidler was essentially at the core of this. William Vidler has several biographic accounts. He was born on 4 May 1758, the tenth and last child of John and Elizabeth Vidler of Battle, who lived on King Street[48]. As a boy he liked reading but was kept from school by ill-health and was apprenticed to his father, a mason and bricklayer who did a lot of work for the Abbey manor estate. The family were Anglican, not Presbyterian and were visited by the Dean, the Rev. Thomas Nairne. He took an interest in William having found that the unschooled son of the stone-mason, "somewhat weak in body"

---

47   ESRO BAT/1446
48   King Street was a former name of High Street

had a mind that was "healthy and avid". But William became even more influenced by the preaching of George Gilbert and he began to lay-preach at the Independent Calvinist Church in 1777.

As noted above he became a Baptist under the influence of Thomas Purdy of Rye in 1780. He also married Charity Sweetenham, William's daughter, on 7 September 1780. They had six children William b. 13 Oct 1782 Ebenezer b. 24 Sep 1784 Charity b. 1 Jan 1787 Rebekah b. 3 Nov 1789 Sarah b. 15 Jan 1792 and Elhanan b. 16 Nov 1793.

Vidler (Figs. 25 and 28) was a powerful preacher, often travelling to villages around Battle and preaching in the open air. He met many insults particularly when he carried out baptismal services in local streams and ponds. Some people from the 'better classes' encouraged these insults and many of the people of Battle were against him. But he is said to have exhibited a constant good humour and wit of reply to enable attacks to sometimes be turned to good account.

During the mid 1780s he read Elhanan Winchester's *'Dialogues on The Universal Restoration'*, published in 1788. Elhanan Winchester was an American who, through John Murray, had adopted the doctrine of Universal Restoration, revived in 1750 by James Relly, a fellow-worker of Whitfield. Winchester had come to England to spread this tenet and in 1787 had drawn together a large and influential congregation at Parliament Court, Artillery Lane, Bishopsgate in London.

Vidler travelled and met doubters of orthodox Baptist doctrine including Andrew Fuller. Vidler met followers of Winchester in Lincolnshire and returned to Battle a strong believer in the universal restoration of all humankind.

In 1791 he undertook further travel among Baptist churches to collect funds for the Battle chapel. He had little success with whittling down the £700 still owed, but the travels allowed him to think a lot, perhaps a bit too much......

He took the opportunity to test *"serious thoughts of the Godhead of Christ and the eternity of hell torments."* He was introduced to Arminian baptists and some Universalists. His own ideas were radical too and by the end of 1792 he had professed Universalism.

"It is long since I wrote anything of the state of my soul" he wrote in his

diary on 22 August 1792. *"I have lately been much stirred up again by reading Mr. Winchester on the final restoration of all things, which doctrine . . . I am constrained to say I believe."*
Locally this led to turmoil in the Baptist Calvinist Church and a huge debate took place on Christmas Day and New Year's Eve 1792 followed by a schism of the Church. A large majority loyally remained with Vidler as Universalists and some later became Unitarians, but 15 people left the church and continued as Particular Baptists.

Figure 25. William Vidler

The Universalist majority kept the chapel. They also kept the £700 debt....which would not be paid off for a very long time. The chapel was renamed after 1793, but the chapel had the legend over the entrance "UNITARIAN CHAPEL – A. D. 1789", which it would not have had from the time of its opening as a Baptist Calvinist Church in early 1790. Walter Burgess of the Unitarian Historical Society, writing in 1928 confirmed that this was a retrospective plaque put in position at a later date during a restoration.
Vidler and his Universalist / Unitarian congregation were duly expelled and excommunicated by the local Baptist association in the summer of 1793. The Minute Book of the Baptist Church at Rye, states:

"July 1st 1793. At a quarterly Church meeting agreed to disown the Church at Battle as a sister church on account of Mr. William Vidler and

many of his people imbibing the erroneous doctrine of Universal Restoration. Also agreed to request Brother Spilstead, Senr., and Sister Ann Howard not to commune with them any longer."

The 1794 records of the Baptist Association state:
  "Mr. Vidler's society at Battle having avowed the error of Universal Restoration was separated from the Association in 1793."

So there was a situation from 1793 where there were two radical Non-conformist churches in Battle. Vidler's Universal Baptists who via Universalism would become Unitarians and the small rump of Particular Baptists. The latter might claim that they were the continuity of the Particular Baptist church formed in 1780, but they had lost their chapel and now had to build again.

As regards William Vidler there is more in the next chapter, but Vidler played a leading role in establishing institutional features Unitarians continue to use to today.

The names of those who joined and left the church from 1780 (when it became Calvinistic Baptist) until 1792 (and leavers after early 1793 when it became Universalist) are available from ESRO. These are kept as Unitarian files and they record the 15 people who continued as Particular Baptists and many others are recorded as either withdrawn or been excluded by 1800 or soon after (leavers names in **bold,** those after the establishment of the Universalist Chapel in ***bold italic***).

There are many still recognisably local names and the full list is given below in recognition of this – maybe a forebear will be spotted. The author for example recognises his own paternal ancestors Cornelius Ford *(sic)* who married Esther Hyland plus his Hounsell maternal great (x n) uncles. The list is in alphabetical order.

1780	Ashby William	To U.S.A.
1783	Ashby Ann	To U.S.A.
1780	Ashdown Elizabeth	now JONES excluded
1792	Austin Sarah	Withdrawn
1781	Backshell Mary	now BURGESS
1789	Backshell Jane	To Diss Norfolk 1790
1780	Badcock William	

1789	Badcock Dinah	now PEPPER
1790	Badcock Mary	
1792	Badcock Thomas	
1785	Barham Arthur	Excluded
1785	Barham Mary	Excluded
1788	*Barron Hugh*	*Excluded 23/10/1797*
1786	Bartholomew Rich.	Excluded
1786	Bartholomew Jeny	From Rye
1786	Bartholomew John	
1788	Barton Joseph	to Codnor Derbyshire Aug 1789
1783	Bavers Richard	Excluded
1792	Beechen John	
1780	Bennet Richard	
1785	Beny Mary	Died (before 1800)
1791	Bine Henry	Dead before 1800
1790	Bishop William	to Lewes
1787	Blundell Elizabeth	
1787	Blundell Stephen Jnr	
1780	Bodle Abraham	
1785	Bray Lucy	
1781	Bretton William	
1788	Bryant Sarah	Excluded 25/6/1792
1787	Burgess Mercy	Died May 1793
1787	Burgess William	
1786	Butcher Elizabeth	Excluded November 1790
1781	Carter Mrs Elizabeth	Died 21/2/1803
1781	Carter Ann	
1783	Carter Mary	
1788	Carter Hannah	now BLUNDELL - by 1800
1780	Chapman Hannah	to Brighton
1781	Chase? Ann	now CUTBERT withdrawn 5/5/1793
1792	Coleman William	Excluded (after 1800)
1786	Cooper Jane	now HOUNSELL excluded
1780	Cramp Judith	Died 28/3/1797
1780	Cramp Samuel	
1785	Cramp Mary	
1792	Cramp Robert	
1792	Cramp Sarah	Dead - before 1800
1788	Creace John	
1788	Creace Mrs.	
1787	Crunden Thomas	Excluded 23/10/1797
1781	Cutbert John	Withdrawn 5/5/1793
1785	Cutbert Sarah Senr.	Died 10/9/1805
1781	Dadswell Robert	to Brighton 1792

1785	Deeprose Elizabeth	
1786	Deeprose John	
1782	Dennet(t) Jane	now SLATTER - before 1800
1788	Dennet(t) Mary	now HOLMES - before 1800
1784	Douch Grace	Excluded (after 1800)
1788	Douch John	
1787	Dunk Henry	Withdrawn by 1800
1787	Dunk Mary	Withdrawn by 1800
1790	Dunk Henry	Died 1792
1785	Easton Jenny	Died February 1793
1787	Easton Stephen	
1792	Easton Edward	
1784	Eaton Charles	
1790	Eaton Thomas	Withdrawn after 1800
1790	Eaton Hannah	Withdrawn after 1800
1792	Eldridge Thomas	Died before 1800
1785	Elliot(t) Deborah	
1785	Elliot(t) Wm.	
1792	Elliot(t) Deborah Jnr.	now HOBBS by 1800
1790	Ellis Mrs.	Withdrawn by 1800
1791	Ford Cornelius	
1784	Foster Ann	
1786	Foster Edward	
1791	Freeman ?	
1780	French Edward	
1783	French Mercy	
1780	Fuller Ann	to Brighton
1780	Fuller Elizabeth	now HAZELDEN withdrawn 1792
1780	Fuller Joseph	Died before 1800
1787	Fuller Stephen	
1788	Gates William	Withdrawn by 1800
1792	Glide/Glydd Samuel	Died before 1800
1792	Glide/Glydd Ann	
1780	Gutsell Samuel	Excluded (after 1800)
1783	Guy Lydia	
1780	Haynes Mary	
1780	Hazelden Ann	Died before 1800
1780	Hazelden Thom.Snr.	Withdrawn by 1800
1792	Hazelden Thom.Jnr.	Withdrawn May 1793
1790	Herod Ann	to Lewes
1787	Hoad Charles	Excluded after 1800
1782	Hobbs Elizabeth	now GUTSELL before 1800
1790	Hobbs Edward	
1790	Hobbs Jasper	Died 19/5/1807 or 1809

1792	Hobbs Martha	now TAYLOR before 1800
1787	Hobden Richard	Withdrawn before 1800
1790	Hobden John	
1791	Hobden Elizabeth	Withdrawn before 1800
1792	Holman Mariah	
1791	Honnysett Hannah	
1792	Hounsell Richard	Withdrawn by 1800
1792	Hounsell William	
1792	Hounsell John	Excluded after 1800
1787	Housley Thomas	Excluded 1/4/1787
1789	Howard William	Excluded 1795 dead by 1800
1792	Howle Susan	Withdrawn by 1800
1781	Hurst Joseph	
1780	Hyland John	
1791	Hyland Esther	now FORD by 1800
1784	Jarvis Mary	now QUAIFE by 1800
1792	Jones William	Withdrawn by 1800
1792	Jones Mary	Died 2/2/1793
1785	Kenward John	
1788	Kenward Thomas	
1789	Kenward Elizabeth	
1786	King William	
1790	King William	of Crowhurst
1790	King Mrs.	Died before 1800
1784	Lacey Thomas	Died September 1788
1792	Langridge Elizabeth	
1792	Langridge James	
1780	Laurence Thomas	
1780	Laurence Ann	
1781	Lusted Abram	
1787	Martin Elizabeth	
1780	Mepham Thomas	
1784	Mepham Mary	Died before 1800
1787	Mepham Hannah	Excluded 27/12/1789
1785	Moon Elizabeth	
1792	Moon John	Died after 1800
1786	Neeve(s) Susannah	Withdrawn 7/5/1793
1788	Neeve(s) Sarah	Withdrawn 5/5/1793
1788	Ne(e)ve(s) Honner	now CRAMP before 1800
1789	Neeve(s) Richard	Excluded before 1800
1792	Ne(e)ve(s) Hannah	
1792	Ne(e)ve(s) George	Died 15/5/1796
1792	Ne(e)ve(s) William	
1789	Page Elizabeth	

Year	Name	Note
1791	Page Thomas	
1792	Page William	
1792	Paine Edward	Died March 1804
1780	Parker John	
1788	Parker Jane	
1785	Pattenden John	
1788	Pattenden Mary	now HOUNDSELL - died bf. 1800
1790	Peckham Mary	of Northiam
1792	Pepper Thomas	
1792	Pepper John	to Rye
1792	Pepper Mary	Withdrawn by 1800
1780	Philcox Mary	
1780	Philcox Thomas	
1791	Philcox Luke	
1790	Pocock Mrs.	
1788	Pollard Sarah	now EATON by 1800
1782	Pugh Ann	to Goodman's Field London 1789
1785	Quaife William	Excluded after 1800
1780	Russell William Snr.	Excluded March 1792
1785	Russell William Jnr.	
1792	Russell Thomas	Withdrawn before 1800
1789	Sands Hannah	Excluded
1792	Sargent Thomas	
1782	Saxby Philadelphia	
1790	Saxby William	
1792	Saxby George	
1790	Selmes Ann	died 13/2/1803
1782	Sinden James	Excluded before 1800
1792	Sinnock Ann	Excluded 17/12/1792
1780	Slatter William Senr.	
1780	Slatter Nicholas	
1780	Slatter George	
1781	Slatter Ann	now WELLER
1787	Slatter Elizabeth	Died 1789
1787	Slatter Samuel	Died 1791
1792	Slatter William Jnr.	
1792	Slatter Jane	
1780	Smith Ann	to Brighton 1793
1781	Smith Richard	to Brighton 1793
1788	Smith Hannah	Withdrawn after 1800
1788	Smith Thomas	Excluded 1796
1780	Spilsted Stephen	
1780	Sweetenham Charity	married William Vidler
1792	Taylor Arthur	

1792	Taylor Frances	now SAXBY after 1800
1787	Thomsett John	Excluded November 1790
1791	Thomsett Elizabeth	Died 8/4/1803
1791	Thomsett John	
1780	Tollhurst Ann	
1785	Venes John	Excluded November 1791
1790	Vidler Elizabeth	Died after 1800
1790	Vidler William	from Rye
1781	W(h)eller Mary	
1781	W(h)eller William	from Rye
1788	Wait Richard	
1790	Wait Elizabeth	Died March 1792
1792	Wait John	Withdrawn before 1800
1792	Weeks John	
1791	White Ruth	
1782	Whiteman Edward	
1786	Wilson Thomas	
1780	Wood Elizabeth	Withdrawn before 1800
1780	Wood Samuel	
1788	Wren(n) John	
1789	Wren(n) Thomas	to Brighton after 1800
1791	Wren(n) Sarah	now BADCOCK after 1800

Some further Baptism records are available from Sussex On-line Parish Clerks[49].

After 1754 Baptists had to marry in Anglican churches and they should be recorded in their parish registers. Baptist marriages became legal again in 1837 if a civil registrar was in attendance.

For burial records see Chapter 6.

---

49 http://www.sussex-opc.org/

Chapter 6
Universalists, then Unitarians 1793-1898

So from early 1793 the Universalists had the chapel (Fig. 26) on Mount Street together with a debt of £700 and William Vidler as their pastor. They were the first regular Church in England to declare for Universalism.

But Vidler was about to move on. He was asked to assist Elhanan Winchester at Parliament Court, Artillery Lane, London, from 9 February 1794. Later that year Winchester returned to America. Vidler became his successor, although he still gave half his time to Battle until November 1796.Ministers after Vidler were[50]

1796- ?	William Thrussell
1819-1828	James Taplin
1828-1843	?
1843-1844	Mr. Hall (of Trowbridge)
1845-1847	George Kenrick
1847-1849	?
1849-1854	Edward Parry
1854-1857	C P Burgess (lay)
1857-1860	?
1861	Frederick Perkins
1861-1880	(time order) Dr. Jeffrey, Wynn Robinson, John Thomas, John Jennings, William Birks, James Bayley, Peter Dean & John Atkinson
1880-1889	Various London Unitarian lay preachers
1889	CLOSED

The Unitarian Chapel was created by a deed of 3 June 1828. It is not clear why there was this delay, perhaps it took some time to evolve from Universalists to Unitarians, or just to do the paperwork, but it

---

50   Taken from: The Surman Index Online, Dr Williams's Centre for Dissenting Studies, http://surman.english.qmul.ac.uk. (lists Congregational ministers, but earlier non-conformists are also listed until Congregational congregations established); the Southern Unitarian Magazine 1888, p112 and the Christian Life of 21 July 1928 pp225-6.

should be noted that the Rules and Regulations of the Unitarian Church at Battle were dated 15 June 1823.

In general the moral character and public behaviour of members was considered to be under the watch of the church. Members considered to somehow be in breach of expected behaviour received visits from 'messengers'. Intoxication, profaneness and non-attendance were the most numerous causes of exclusion, but one non-attending member gave the reason for his absence *'that he had been informed the pastor cut the bread instead of breaking it'*. A plaintive note was added to the minute *'The pastor always breaks the bread'*. One member *'liked going to the play-house'* and was therefore excluded.

In 1843 several repairs to the roof, floors and windows had been done and new iron gates and new doors fitted. A Mr Hall of Trowbridge was asked to come on trial as minister at a salary of £35 per annum, but he left soon afterwards as the congregation was unable to pay him.

George Kenrick came as minister in 1845 and was apparently much appreciated by his congregation. He worked hard to get Holy Communion services to be well attended, trying several different formats, all to little avail as these services were seemingly not popular.

However the Sunday School was, and nearly 150 children attended and for over 100 of these this was almost the only place in Battle that the poor could obtain any education. A Mr J Crouch who was a member offered to build a school room for £100, but as there was still a debt of £69 on the building it was thought right to clear that before any further building took place.

Edward Parry who arrived in 1849 made a greater impression on Battle. At that time Battle had a house levy of £4 per house collected for the Dean of St. Mary's. (The only other place in the country with a similar collection was St. Albans.). Mr. Parry refused to pay this and was summoned before the magistrates. They issued a warrant for him to pay with an added 10s costs. No one would collect this until the magistrates forced the local constable to do so, threatening to fine him £5 if he did not. He seized 25 books which were sold to a person from Hastings on the Market Green. The buyer experienced 'much indignation and excitement'.

Fig. 26 A photograph held at ESRO of the Unitarian Chapel – it is of course the same building as shown in Fig. 24

Parry also tried to claim a vote on the freehold of the chapel, but was unable to produce the deeds, which were found 6 or 7 years later in the possession of a Mr Munn of Tenterden.... Parry worked for a pittance and encouraged the development of a choir.

He left in 1854 and for the next three years a young member of the Freethinking Christian Movement, Mr C P Burgess volunteered to conduct services. After this there was a succession of ministers and finally cover from London Unitarian lay-preachers. But the congregation dwindled and closure became inevitable in 1889.

In 1888 it was recorded in the Southern Unitarian Magazine that in

1854, when a Government inspector called to survey the town burial grounds, 20% of the Unitarian burial ground was still available for burials which were occurring at a rate of 8 per annum. It was incidentally noted that 2 burials per year were taking place in the smaller burial ground of the Zion Chapel. This relatively obscure report was to be key planning evidence many years later, but the two graveyards were clearly marked **GY** on the 1:2500 OS map of 1873-79 (detail from this copied as Fig. 27) which should have raised suspicions on the local Planning Committee.

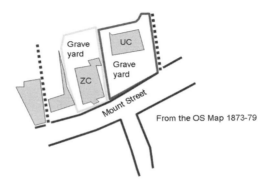

Figure 27. The Graveyards of the Zion Baptist and Unitarian Chapels

Due to the dwindling congregations and its closure for worship the chapel was sold under a Charity Commissioners Scheme dated 1 October 1897, with the proceeds paid to the British and Foreign Unitarian Association. It formally finally closed in 1898, but to prevent the disposal of the building and site, they were purchased by an old member of the chapel, Miss Lucy Tagart, who did not live locally. She let it from 1898 to the Mountjoy Institute to be used for the recreation and education of young people. She died in 1928. In her will, dated 20 September 1925, she appointed Unitarian trustees to administer the chapel, but ownership of it passed to her heirs with the rest of her property.

In 1928 the Mountjoy Institute was given notice to quit. After this it was in the hands of the Unitarian Trustees who allowed use of the building for a variety of purposes, including as a store room during WW2, until its final sale in 1946. Again it is not clear who benefited from this sale, possibly the surprised distant heirs of Miss Tagart.

Presumably it stood empty and unused until it was sold once again in 1957 to a dairyman, who demolished the chapel and covered over the burial ground without any exhumations. No burial registers seemed to have survived, so that the tombstones were the only record of burials up to 1862, when burials ceased as the graveyard was full. There was also an Order in Council that year for the cessation of burials at all the churches in the town. From that time forwards all Battle burials took place at the new cemetery on Marley Lane.

The depot was subsequently sold to Unigate Dairies in 1961 who purchased it in good faith. Unigate re-sold the site in 1979 and the new owner obtained outline planning permission for the erection of flats.

Soon afterwards it was proven (see above) that the site incorporated a disused burial ground and the development did not take place. The story of this, the sale of the whole site to the Zion Baptist Church and their management of the site since then will be covered in the next chapter 7, but Mrs M J Hadaway of Sevenoaks researched this in 1986 and her account and lists of members and burials at the site are recorded on the Sussex On-line Parish Clerks website[51].

In view of his importance in the events of the early 1790s in Battle it is worth recording a bit more detail about William Vidler once he left Battle for the wider Unitarian world.

William Vidler (4 May 1758 - 23 August 1816) became a well respected Universalist and Unitarian preacher and publisher and together with Richard Wright Vidler played a significant role in establishing institutions which Unitarians continue to use today. Vidler had strengthened his ties with Elhanan Winchester in the early 1790s and in 1794 he became his assistant at the Universalist Chapel in Parliament Court, Artillery Lane, London[52]. Winchester

---

51 http://www.sussex-opc.org/ParishDetails/EastSussex/Battle/BattleUnitarian.htm
52 Now Sandys Row Synagogue

who was American returned to the USA later that year and Vidler became his successor. He had become a famed preacher and crowds attended to hear him.

In 1797 he published a magazine called initially the Universalist Miscellany. He edited this for many years. In 1798 he was involved in revising a publication of a New Testament translated from the Original Greek, which has been described as 'a useful curiosity' in that it presented dialogues dramatically. In 1804 he founded the Unitarian Evangelical Society and from 1806 was travelling widely for the Unitarian Fund. He seems to have had great intellectual energy. Even in later life he was learning Latin for the first time and reading J B Priestley's works.

Figure 28. William Vidler in later life

Vidler became exceedingly corpulent (Fig 28). He always booked two seats when journeying by coach. Returning to London from Wisbech in 1808 to see his dying wife, the coach in which he was travelling fell down a steep bank. He was injured and never fully recovered and preached thereafter sitting down.

He went to live in West Ham and died on 23 August 1816. He is buried in the graveyard of the former Unitarian Chapel at Hackney in East London. He said of himself: 'Whatever changes I have gone through, whatever errors I may have held, I have this satisfaction, that I have ever held fast my integrity'.

Chapter 7
Battle Baptists (1780) - 1793 – 2011

The early formative history of this Church from 1780 to 1793 has been previously discussed in Chapter 5.

With the acrimonious split in 1793 from William Vidler's Calvinistic Baptists, soon to be Universalists and then Unitarians the 15 continuing members of the Particular Baptists faced the daunting task of literally re-building their church spiritually and physically. To follow this journey we fortunately have access to a book written by the Rev. F W Butt-Thompson in 1909 for much, but not all, of our information after 1793.

The members were meeting in houses again. They had soon grown from the 15 souls, presumably mainly by further defections from the Universalists, to be big enough to have a minister of their own and a Mr. J. Brown came to them from Norfolk between 1793 and 1794.

There was no replacement minister immediately after this, but in 1795, Sergeant Burton, of the Warwickshire Militia (presumably based at the Battle Barracks on Whatlington Road) and a Mr. Bondergham (sent out by the Church at Folkestone) covered the absence. The Rev. J. Davies, from Ramsey, Huntingdonshire, then took over as Minister in 1796.

From 1798 to 1803 they rented a piece of land, set back from Mount Street, but with a right of way to the road. The land was described as triangular in shape, 40m (125 ft) long, and from 10m (33ft) to 2m (6 ft) in width, in area about 177m^2 (7 rods). This would have been a most awkward piece of land to build on, but in 1800 whilst the land was still rented, a Meeting House of wood was constructed, "a neat and comfortable place," holding some 200 people. This was erected by carpenter James Inskipp, Junr., and John Longley. The tithe map of 1840 (Fig. C4) shows that this may have been an L-shaped building, which may be how it fitted on this odd shaped piece of land.

Their accounts were as follows:

	£	s	d
Meeting House by Estimate	61	14	9
Pulpit and Appendages	4	3	5
Hat Pins, etc.	0	12	7
New Stools and altering old	3	9	5½
Front Gates and Fence	1	5	0½
Pal'd Fence in the Yard	5	7	3
Bricklayers' Work, etc.	30	11	3

It would be interesting to know where the hat pins etc. were used. However for the sum of £107 8s 9d, they had a building of their own for the first time since 1793. In January 1801 the accounts were paid by Messrs. Ffoord, Sargent, and others on behalf of the Church. In 1803, the leasehold of the land on which the wooden Meeting House stood was bought on behalf of the church by Mr Spilstead,Snr. and Mr. Ffoord[53].

The Rev. Davies left the church in 1802. Sinnock's memoir reports that he fell into 'disgrace' and that the church dismissed him. So after a short time without a pastor, Mr. J. Bagnall[54] became the Pastor sometime in 1803. He had been a former member of the Church and also a local preacher whilst in the militia and barracked at Battle. Returning to former friends, he did good work for a few months. However in 1804 the Wesleyan Church was founded in Battle and Bagnall moved to it, taking some followers. This appears to have been secondary to yet another schism[55] and no new pastor arrived for the Baptists until the end of 1806.

In November 1806, the Rev. J. Kingsmill arrived. He was popular and stayed for 13 years, until he died on 6th January 1819.

In 1810 the freehold of the Meeting House land was finally formally conveyed from Messrs. Spilstead and Ffoord to the Church at a cost

---

53 By the way the author can find no family connection between himself and Mr John Ffoord, who was a baker.

54 Richard Sinnock's memoir states that Bagnall had been in the Militia and stationed at Battle and whilst there had been baptised

55 Sinnock's wife commented that she did not think him a sound preacher and Sinnock describes Bagnall as having imbibed Antinomian doctrine (that by faith and the dispensation of grace a Christian is released from the obligation of adhering to any moral law).

of £21. It is described in the deed as "part of messuage formerly known as the 'Rose and Crown' ". The Church bought the land via a co-operative with nearly every member paying a portion of the price. Butt-Thompson writes: The Trust Deed declared the place to be for

" *the Pious and Religious Exercise and purposes of the members of the said Society or Congregation, who should hold believe and maintain The Tenets and Doctrines of three equal and distinct persons in the Godhead, Father, Son, and Spirit. Election before time to holiness here and glory hereafter. Justification alone by the imputed Righteousness of Jesus Christ. The Salvation of the Elect only. The Resurrection of the Dead. The Last Judgement. Eternal Life for the Righteous and endless death to the wicked.*"

These members (who became Trustees) were:
William Spilstead, Senr., Ewhurst, Yeoman.
John Ffoord (written "fford"), Battle, Baker.
George Sargent, Battle, Draper
John Bartholomew, Westfield, Yeoman.
William Mainwaring, Burwash, Clocksmith.
Luke Philcox, Battle, Cordwainer.
Thomas Dawes, Rye, Turner.
Edward French, Crowhurst, Yeoman.
James Kingsmill, Battle, Gentleman.
Elizabeth Ffoord (wife of John Ffoord).
Ann Sargent (wife of George Sargent).
Richard Hounsell, Battle, Labourer.
William Knight, Battle, Tallow Chandler.
Mary Sinnock (wife of Richard Sinnock, Gent.).
Elizabeth Newington (wife of John Newington, Gent.).
Elizabeth Page, Battle, Spinster.
Mary Philcox, Battle, Widow.
Elizabeth Wood, Battle, Widow.
Samuel Willis, Burwash, Labourer.
Thomas Pavey, Burwash, Labourer.
Richard Hobden, Penhurst, Labourer.
James Sinden, Warbleton, Labourer.
Thomas Housley, Robertsbridge, Cordwainer.

This wooden meeting house was used for worship for 23 years, after which it was used for Sunday Schools until 1869. The Chapel members asked Jonathan Jenner who was auditing their accounts to be responsible for its sale by public auction. The building does not appear on the OS 1:2,500 map of 1873-79 so it must have been demolished by then. Its site was sold in 1886. Florence Cottages, now on Rue de Bayeux and attached to the Roman Catholic Church, were built on the land some years later in 1897.

In 1799 a Mr. Richard Sinnock (b.1740) built a house on Mount Street (Fig.31), next to the Baptist Church which he attended . He must have leased or purchased the whole of or much of 'the messuage formerly known as the 'Rose and Crown' before 1798 as the deeds of his house's land also refer to this. He was one of the 15 representatives of the original Baptist Church (his relative, Ann Sinnock, was one of those excluded on 17/12/1792).

Sinnock had run a cordwaining business in Hastings in 1762, but moved to London in 1785 in order to join a dissenting sect (no church in Hastings provided what he wanted), he then moved on to Guildford, but then moved back to Sussex. He did not wish to live in Hastings again as at that time there was no Dissenters House, so he built his house in Battle in 1799. He was clearly of some substance, via his previous business and had obviously retained local real estate interests. In about 1800 he leased one of his old shops in Hastings to be a meeting house and later in 1805 he bought some land in Hastings for the sum of £400 on which the Croft Chapel was built. He has left a fascinating memoir (lodged at ESRO).

In June 1820 Mr. J. Puntis arrived from Stepney Academy to be minister and he was so successful that in September of that year a larger building was commenced. This is the present chapel, *"plain, neat, modernised and commodious,"* opened in February 1821 with an indenture dated 3rd April 1821 consisting of the chapel and site managed by a body of Trustees. A copy of the indenture in 6 parts is held by Battle Baptists.

The signatures of each Trustee and the seals at the base of the Indenture are copied below in Fig.29.

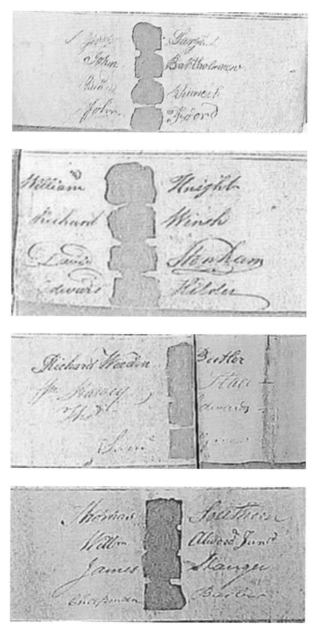

Figure 29. Copies of signatures - courtesy Battle Baptist Church

These Trustees whose signatures appear above, appointed on 3rd April 1821, were:

George Sargent.
John Bartholomew.
Richard Sinnock, Battle, Gentleman.
John Ffoord.
William Knight.
Richard Winch, Crowhurst, Farmer.
David Stonham, Rye, Draper.
Edward Hilder, Rye, Ironmonger.
Richard Weedon Butler, Rye, Surgeon.
William Harvey Staco, Folkestone, Miller.
Thomas Edwards, Folkestone, Draper.
Samuel Green, Sevenoaks, Builder.
Thomas Southern, Sevenoaks, Distiller.
William Atwood, Junr., Farningham, Shopkeeper.
James Stanger, Maidstone, Ironmonger.
Chapman Barber

Richard Sinnock had clearly approved of Mr Puntis and prompted by Mrs Sargent, the wife of George Sargent (a nephew of Sinnock's wife) had generously given the land to the north side of his new house on which to build this new permanent chapel. This land is described

"All that piece of land situate in the Borough of Mount Joy in the Parish of Battle, abutting north on a Chapel and Burying Ground in the possession of a Society called Unitarians: south on a house and premises belonging to Richard Sinnock east on the Public Road leading to London[56]; and west on a garden belonging to Sir Godfrey Webster."

This is where the Zion Chapel (Figs.30, 32 and 34) was built in 1820-1821 and stands to this day. A small burying ground was rear of the new chapel, which itself had a close frontage onto Mount Street.

William Sinnock survived his wife Mary (Williams) whom he had

---

56 This was 'The Mount' now known as Mount Street. The road to London ran
    through Whatlington to join the road from Rye (which itself ran along the
    ridge through Brede and Udimore)

married in St Clement's Church, Hastings, on 27th April 1763. She died on 24th August 1817. In his will of 1823 he requested that George Sargent, his executor arrange that he be buried at the FRONT of the Zion Chapel, clearly not at the rear in the small burying ground. He died on 2nd November 1827 at the age of 87. No burial slab has survived, it may be that this was lost at the time of the demolition of the porch of the Zion Chapel.

Figure 30. Zion Baptist Chapel, Mount Street

Richard Sinnock seems to have had no direct heirs on his death and his estate passed mainly to his nephew Richard Sinnock Middlemas. Sinnock's house appears to have been sold after his death and on the tithe map of 1840 it is shown to belong to one William Weston.
It still stands and after being bought by the 5th Earl of Ashburnham in 1882 is now the fine wood clad Presbytery of the Catholic Church called 'The Hollies' (Fig.31). Would Richard Sinnock have approved?......It would seem very doubtful. It is also interesting to note that an Ann Sinnock (who may have been Richard Sinnock's nephew's wife) was buried in Battle Unitarian burial ground in 1827. The new building was registered at the Diocese of Chichester for worship as a Congregation of Protestant Dissenters in the possession

of George Sargent[57] on 20th February 1821. Seven days later on Tuesday, 27th February 1821, the new Meeting House called Zion Chapel, belonging to the Baptist denomination, was opened for public worship.

Figure 31. The Hollies – Richard Sinnock's old house, now the Catholic Presbytery

"Rules of Interment in Zion Burying Ground" were drawn up. The burial fee was to be four shillings and this would be used to keep the ground in order and mend the fences. Every burial was to be paid for "save the minister, or any member of his family." Also it was to be open to "persons unbaptised, who therefore are not entitled to what is called 'Christian Burial'".

The new Trust Deed declared that the Meeting House and small Burying Ground were;

"for the use and benefit of the Society or Congregation of Protestant Dissenters called Particular Baptists, now and hereafter assembling at the said Meeting House and premises, maintaining the doctrines of the One living and True Lord, Three equal Persons in the Godhead, Eternal and

---

personal Election, Original sin and Particular Redemption, Free Justification by the imputed righteousness of Christ, Regeneration, Conversion, and Sanctification by the Spirit and grace of God, the moral law a rule of life and conduct to all believers, the final perseverance of the Saints, the resurrection of the body to eternal life, the future judgement, the eternal happiness of the righteous and everlasting misery to such as die impenitent, and the practice of Baptism by immersion to such only as are of years of understanding upon their own confession of repentance towards God and faith in our Lord Jesus Christ."

They loved their words in those days - note the barb to the Unitarians.

Mr. William Garner followed Mr. Puntis as Minister in February 1827, following which the membership increased greatly, some walking in to services from Ashburnham, Darwell Hole, Netherfield, Penhurst, Pont's Green, Vinehall, Whatlington and Wood's Dale.

The Rev. S. Stennett was the next pastor 1835. The year after that an event occurred which those of us who lived in Battle in October 1987 and who experienced the 'Great Storm' can empathise with. The Great Hurricane of 29th November 1836 ripped over England. It was truly widespread and houses were torn apart, barns shattered, and public buildings destroyed. The Zion Chapel was so badly damaged that the cost of repairs could not be afforded by the congregation.

An appeal was made for financial help, but when an answer came from their neighbours at Rye it stated in turn that they had hoped for assistance from Battle, for their own place had been partially un-roofed in the storm. Somehow the church managed this crisis.

In fact two years later they opened a branch at Netherfield, the Sabbath School and Place of Worship. The Diocese records state that this was registered for worship on 2 October 1822 as a Congregation of Protestant Dissenters in a building known as Netherfield Sunday School Room, Netherfield, Battle, in occupation of George Sargent[58]. However this was to be sold under a Charity Commissioners scheme on 23 June 1885, with the proceeds being added to the receipts from the sale of the old wooden meeting place and its site to help fund new school rooms at the rear of the Zion Chapel (see below)

---

58   WSRO, EpII/25/3

Figure 32. Old photograph of Zion Chapel showing the old porch. From the frontispiece of Butt-Thompson's book , looking north up Mount Street[59].

From 1837 Baptist marriages became legal again if a civil registrar was in attendance. Between 1754 and 1837 Baptists had to marry in Anglican churches and these marriages should be recorded in their registers (Richard Sinnock's marriage was an example).

Membership had risen to 64 by 1841 when Stennett left to be replaced by the Rev. Robert Grace. The full list of pastors will be found at the end of the chapter; so from this point forwards rather than list the events of each pastor-ship it is probably better to list the major events.

From 1854 the Government had been trying to close the town's various burial grounds which were nearly full. Several closure Orders in Council were received by the three town churches with burial grounds and by 1862 the burial grounds around all of the town's churches, including the small Zion Chapel ground, were closed by order of the Privy Council and a new public cemetery was opened off Marley Lane.

---

59   This must be from after 1899 as this is when the buttresses were added. The porch has now been removed. The luxuriant tree is growing in the Unitarian burying ground.

The decade 1870-80 seems to have been one of the most prosperous ones for the Zion Chapel since the days of William Vidler. The church was nearing its centenary (of foundation as Free Calvinists that is). On March 3rd 1875 members of the Congregation calling themselves 'The Mutual Improvement Society' gave a concert, the programme of which is reproduced below (Fig.34). Most of the farmers around the town were members, and some of the most wealthy inhabitants were found worshipping in "Zion".

In 1873 the practice of admitting unbaptised believers to the membership was made lawful by a new rule of the Church. It may have been this move that led to the foundation of the Strict Baptist group which met at Langton House (see Chapter 10). On the other hand this decision also appears to have led to membership from May 1873 of the Jenner and Mannington families who had been active attenders since 1869. Jonathan Jenner in particular was very active and became Chapel treasurer and later deacon in 1873.

The question of adult baptism arose again in 1880 and the Church re-instituted the requirement that adult baptism was a pre-requisite of membership. Clearly some members, including Jonathan Jenner and his family who had been accepted after 1873 and had had prior infant baptism were uncomfortable with this and the Jenners were amongst the 22 members who left and formed a Congregational Church.

Battle Baptists also had some branch mission stations, notably at Whatlington, which had closed due to competition from a new Methodist Chapel (the latter is the white chapel that now sells heating stoves on the A21) and at Netherfield. In 1886 its Netherfield Mission Station, the last of the branches of the Battle Baptist Church, was sold to Robertson Street Congregational Church of Hastings, for £65. The money was reserved for the building of a new Sunday School which was built to the rear of the church. In the same year the old wooden chapel and its land was sold and the money used to renovate Zion Chapel, but in 1899 there was the considerable expense of buttressing the church, the results of which can be seen today.

In 1906 there was a local move to unite the Baptist and Congregational churches, mainly it seems as both churches were struggling to fund their pastors, but it was found to be impossible after 'full and frank' discussions.

The Baptist congregation continued to wane and just before the Rev. F W Butt-Thompson was appointed in 1908 it had dropped to 27. Things struggled on often with support from neighbouring churches.

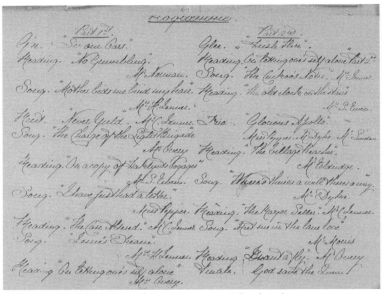

Figure 33. The Mutual Improvement Society's programme - courtesy Battle Baptist Church

When WW2 broke out the schoolroom was taken over by the Army for the billeting of troops. The Military paid the Church five shillings per week. During the war special permits had to be obtained from the local food office for the Church Anniversary and Good Friday teas and these supplies were supplemented with food saved by members from their own rations. In 1942, the Church railings were requisitioned for the war effort. During this time the membership was 38 and between 1942 and 1945 alternate weekly services were held in either the Baptist or Congregational Church.

The Dean of Battle, the Rev. J. Darby, preached in the Baptist Church for the very first time in 1975. Although inter-church relations were improving in the 1970s things were still not generally very good for

Battle Baptists. On top of this significant major repairs were required to the Zion Chapel towards the end of the decade. Some thought the best action would be to disband. They were lean years for the Chapel and membership was rarely higher than 35. But things were about to improve.

In the previous chapter we have seen how the Unitarian Chapel had waned in membership and closed. Then its building was eventually demolished to make way for a dairy depot. This depot was built in 1953 over the old burial ground, surprisingly without any exhumation of remains. Eyewitnesses reported bull-dozing of the surviving gravestones to the side of the Zion Chapel. Unigate Dairies bought the dairy distribution unit in 1961, in good faith, but closed and re-sold the site in 1979, but then nothing happened.

In 1979 the wife of the Baptist pastor went on to the site and claimed it for the Lord's work. Tragically her hopes appeared to be dashed when, just a few weeks later, her young husband Pastor John Halliday was killed. He had only been in post five months.

In 1980 E J T Tyler of the Battle and District Historical Society recorded details from all the old tombstones from the dairy site that he could find and read (they had been shunted to one side) and a typed transcript of the inscriptions is held at ESRO[60] .

In September 1980 Dennis Nolan was asked to be Lay Pastor to the church (he was to be ordained in 1983). He was convinced that if the Baptist Church were to survive then the site of the former dairy would be needed for expansion.

In January 1982 a "For Sale" board was erected on the site. At a church meeting the few members present agreed to offer £6,000 towards the project, but this was not enough to buy it. There then followed three years of frustration. Plans to redevelop the dairy site as a block of six flats were approved in 1982. Protests were made because of local knowledge of the presence of the now unmarked graves, but at that stage no supporting documentary evidence could be found in proof.

Between 1980 and 1984 church membership grew. £20,000 was offered for the site. This offer was rejected. In 1984 the church was informed by its solicitors that the site had been "irrevocably sold" for redevelopment which would start within weeks, but the development did not start.

Figure 34. Zion Chapel gallery

In January 1985, after extensive research, the burial ground closure Order in Council dated 1862 was found. Review of the old 1:2500 OS map of 1873-1878 (Fig.27) also shows graveyards clearly belonging to the old Unitarian Chapel as well as a small graveyard north of the Zion Chapel itself. There was also the report from the 'Southern Unitarian' of 1888 previously mentioned, which included a photograph of the old Unitarian Chapel, with many gravestones clearly visible.

There was really no doubt at all that there was a burial ground, but the developers still seemed undeterred and in March 1985 gave public notice of intention to exhume human remains.

By April 1985 the Home Office ruled that the entire site must be cleared of graves before development could take place. Dennis Nolan, now the full time minister, managed to make an offer of £30,000 for the site. This was rejected, but an anonymous benefactor enabled a higher bid of £45,000 to be made, only to discover that in the meantime yet another developer had purchased the site and new planning permission had also been granted to develop the area as apartments.

In December 1985 another generous gift was made to finally enable the site to be purchased from the developers for £57,000, considerably more than the £160 paid for the same land in 1789. Between 1985 and 1989 various sets of plans were drawn up and discussed by the church.

In 1989 church members spent two months working on site to exhume 108 sets of human remains by hand, before building work could take place. Re-interment of the remains took place in the Marley Lane Cemetery where a commemorative stone marks the site.

Since 1987 the church has used Claverham Community College as the venue for most of its Sunday morning meetings as the total size of its congregation is too big for the Zion Chapel. A second pastor was called in 1989 and a manse near the church purchased.

In December 1989 the foundations for phase 1 of a new development on the north side of the chapel fronting on to Mount Street were laid and "The Manna House", a meeting place for a variety of activities, was opened in December 1990. 2002 saw phase two of the development project. The 1880 Victorian school hall to the rear of the chapel was demolished and the "Bayeux Centre" a large facility for children and young persons plus a prayer room, office, resource room and a second kitchen was opened in November 2002 (Fig.35). This has provided the church with premises fit to enable it to continue more than 200 years of Baptist worship to God and service to the local community. In 2006 they bought another small neighbouring plot of land for further development and in 2011 they are building an extension to the Manna House.

The author would like to further acknowledge at this point the on-line documents about this Church by the Rev. Dennis Nolan and the help given by John Southam of the Battle Baptists.

94

Figure 35. Early 2011. The Manna House on the left and the Bayeux
Centre back right viewed from Mountjoy. There is now a small
extension to the Manna House.

Pastors of Battle Baptist Church

1780-1792	W. Vidler
1793-1794	J. Brown
1796-1802	J. Davies
1803-1805	J. Bagnall
1806-1819	J. Kinghill (Sinnock's memoir says Kingsmill)
1820-1827	J. Puntis
1827-1835	W. Garner
1835-1841	B. Stennet
1842-1849	R. Grace
1849-1853	P. Perkins
1853-1856	J. Maurice
1857-1859	J. Pulman
1860-1863	C.G. Brown
1863-1872	G. Veals
1873-1875	G. Wright
1875-1895	J. Howes
1895-1897	G.B.. Richardson

1899-1902	O.W. Screech
1903-1906	J.R. Hewison
1907-1910	F.W. Butt-Thompson
1911-1921	P. Stanley
1921-1923	J. Gotham
1925-1928	H.J. Dale
1932-1933	T.O. Weller
1942-1946	H. Anderton
1946-1957	S. Kerr
1959-1963	H. Emmott
1963-1968	S.W. Gowley
1969-1976	J. Hunt
1979	J Halliday
1980-1983	D Nolan acted as lay Pastor
1983-date	D Nolan

Chapter 8
Methodists 1804 – 2011

Figure 36. Battle Methodist Chapel, built 1826 and extended 1886/7

John Wesley is largely credited, along with his brother Charles Wesley, as founding the Methodist movement which began when he took to open-air preaching. Wesley helped to organize and form societies of Christians throughout Britain and Ireland as small groups that developed personal accountability, discipleship and religious instruction among members.

His great contribution was to appoint itinerant preachers, some of whom he ordained himself or who were ordained by others[61] and in addition unordained lay-preachers who travelled to evangelise and care for people in these societies. Many of the lay-preachers did not move around very much and it is notable that local lay-preachers are still extensively used within the Methodist Church.

His unconventional use of church policy put him at odds with many

---

61 This was a policy that put him at odds with many in the Church of England.

within the Church of England, although throughout his life Wesley remained within the Church of England and insisted that his movement was well within the bounds of the Anglican tradition. Toward the end of his life he was widely respected as "the best loved man in England."

Because of his charitable nature he died poor, leaving as the result of his life's work 135,000 members and 541 itinerant preachers under the name "Methodist". It has been said that "when John Wesley was carried to his grave, he left behind him a good library of books, a well-worn clergyman's gown," and the Methodist Church.

After John Wesley's death in March 1791 his followers broke away from the Anglican Church and formed the Wesleyan Church. In this respect it differed somewhat from the other Non-conformist churches, which derived more from the Presbyterian / Calvinist tradition which had had links with Anglicanism in the time of the Commonwealth, but had since separated and become more radical with further diverging churches.

Almost as usual at the end of the 18th and the start of the 19th centuries, which were times of intense discussion about religion, there were disagreements about interpretations of the Bible. These led to fragmentation of the Wesleyan Church with the Methodist New Connexion being formed in 1797, the Primitive Methodist Church in 1807, the Bible Christians in 1815, the Wesleyan Protestant Methodist Church in 1827, the Wesleyan Methodist Association in 1834 and the Wesleyan Reformers in 1847.

The last three groups to be formed amalgamated in 1857 to form the United Methodist Free Church. In 1907 the Methodist New Connexion, the Bible Christians and the United Free Methodist Church joined together to form the United Methodist Church. Finally the Wesleyans, the Primitive Methodists and the United Methodists came together in 1932 to form The Methodist Church. So almost all Methodist sects were united by 1934.

During the period of fragmentation the Wesleyan Church was clearly the largest Methodist group and the Wesleyan Church was always predominant in East Sussex. It was a Wesleyan Church which was founded in Battle in 1804 and the members rented rooms in which to hold their services

In 1803, Mr. J. Bagnall had become the Pastor of the Zion Baptist Church. He had been a member of this Church before and a local preacher, when in the Militia at Battle, but had moved to Leicestershire. The Battle Baptist church asked him to return, which he did, but soon afterwards, in 1804, the Wesleyan Church was founded in the town. Bagnall moved to this church, taking with him some of his followers and conducted the Wesleyan services in a hired room. He had obviously upset the Baptists and Richard Sinnock records in his memoir that his character turned out *'so very bad that those who had supported him saw their error and left him'*. However we know no more than this about the affair. No records appear to have survived from this early period of 1804 but a later Hastings Circuit Book is lodged with ESRO and names the members of the Battle Church from 1822. At that time there was only the one Preacher to cover the whole circuit. There were 20 Battle members in the 1822 Circuit list :

Joseph and Martha Burgifs
Mary Marchant
William Metcalf
Rebecca Richards
Mary Catt
Robert, Elizabeth, Ann and Eleanor Hyland
William Gibbs
Edward Cresey
John Crouch
John and Elizabeth Pankhurst
James Meek
Benjamin Bran
Spencer Noakes
Benedicta Bury
Jane Waite

Residents of Battle will again recognise some local family names. Similar lists are available at about two yearly intervals, with 17 members in 1824, 26 in 1826 including Charles and Henry Foord[62] and 24 in 1830. After that once again little information of note is available. More recently numbers in membership rose to 48 in 1935 before declining again to the mid 20s in the 1980s, then gradually rising again towards 50 by 2011.

Surprisingly there is little on record about the building of the Wesleyan Chapel on Lower Lake in 1826 (Fig.36), but the front part of the chapel was constructed at that time, with no porch. The land may have been cheap as it was near the tannery[63]. This was before the railway came to Battle, but when it did he Railway Hotel was built (Fig.37). The latter is now the Senlac pub.

Figure 37. Looking up Battle Hill, early 1900s. The Wesleyan Chapel on the right, with the Railway Hotel on the left and the tannery in the distance

A fortuitous lodging at ESRO is of a scrapbook which contains quarterly membership tickets for the Crouch, Eldridge, Plumb, Putland and Beaney families from 1827, just after the Chapel was opened, up until September 1876 when the chapel was about to be extended (Fig.38). The first ticket was for William Crouch.

---

62 Related to the author
63 Tanneries were notably pungent places to be near.

A note from the Wesleyan Chapel Committee which is dated 6 February 1874 (Fig.39) confirms permission to spend £410 on the chapel extensions. This is stuck into the front of an early minute book, which again surprisingly contains little other historic information. It does however appear that it took some time to get the resources to build as this was not completed for over 10 years. The 1886/7 extension comprised a large airy and well windowed house attached to the rear of the chapel and a good sized porch to the front. Foundation stones for the new extensions were laid by Mr William H Atkin, Mrs. John Gallop. Mrs J Bonsor and Mrs Jabez Stace. All are dated 12th October 1887.

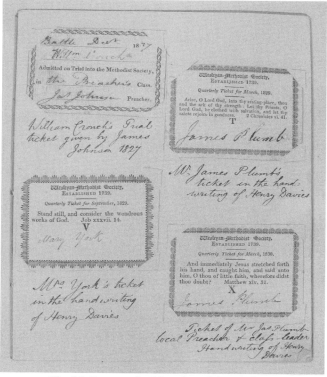

Fig.38 Quarterly Membership Tickets

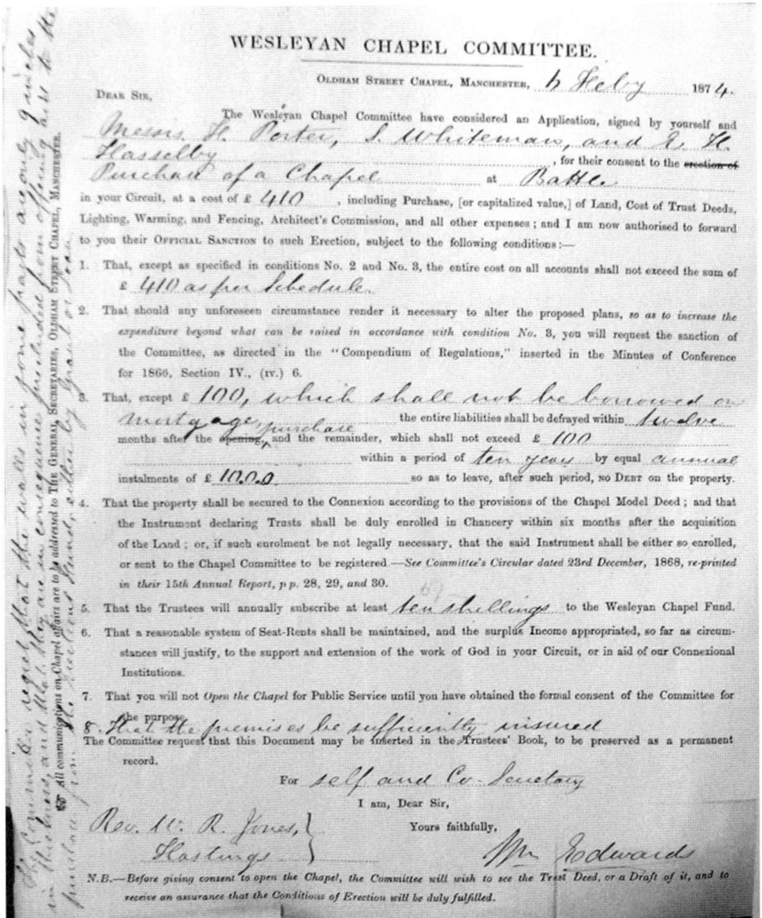

WESLEYAN CHAPEL COMMITTEE.

OLDHAM STREET CHAPEL, MANCHESTER, 6 Feby 1874.

DEAR SIR,

The Wesleyan Chapel Committee have considered an Application, signed by yourself and Messrs. H. Porter, S. Whiteman, and E. H. Hasselby, for their consent to the ~~erection of~~ Purchase of a Chapel at Battle in your Circuit, at a cost of £ 410, including Purchase, [or capitalized value,] of Land, Cost of Trust Deeds, Lighting, Warming, and Fencing, Architect's Commission, and all other expenses; and I am now authorised to forward to you their OFFICIAL SANCTION to such Erection, subject to the following conditions:—

1. That, except as specified in conditions No. 2 and No. 3, the entire cost on all accounts shall not exceed the sum of £ 410 as per Schedule.
2. That should any unforeseen circumstance render it necessary to alter the proposed plans, *so as to increase the expenditure beyond what can be raised in accordance with condition No. 3*, you will request the sanction of the Committee, as directed in the "Compendium of Regulations," inserted in the Minutes of Conference for 1866, Section IV., (IV.) 6.
3. That, except £ 100, which shall not be borrowed on mortgage, the entire liabilities shall be defrayed within twelve months after the ~~opening~~ purchase, and the remainder, which shall not exceed £ 100 within a period of ten years by equal annual instalments of £ 10.0.0 so as to leave, after such period, no DEBT on the property.
4. That the property shall be secured to the Connexion according to the provisions of the Chapel Model Deed; and that the Instrument declaring Trusts shall be duly enrolled in Chancery within six months after the acquisition of the Land; or, if such enrolment be not legally necessary, that the said Instrument shall be either so enrolled, or sent to the Chapel Committee to be registered.—*See Committee's Circular dated 23rd December, 1868, re-printed in their 15th Annual Report, p.p. 28, 29, and 30.*
5. That the Trustees will annually subscribe at least ten shillings to the Wesleyan Chapel Fund.
6. That a reasonable system of Seat-Rents shall be maintained, and the surplus Income appropriated, so far as circumstances will justify, to the support and extension of the work of God in your Circuit, or in aid of our Connexional Institutions.
7. That you will not *Open the Chapel* for Public Service until you have obtained the formal consent of the Committee for the purpose.
8. That the premises be sufficiently insured

The Committee request that this Document may be inserted in the Trustees' Book, to be preserved as a permanent record.

For self and Co-Secretary

I am, Dear Sir,

Yours faithfully,

Wm Edwards

Rev. W. R. Jones, Hastings

N.B.—Before giving consent to open the Chapel, the Committee will wish to see the Trust Deed, or a Draft of it, and to receive an assurance that the Conditions of Erection will be duly fulfilled.

All communications on Chapel affairs are to be addressed to THE GENERAL SECRETARIES, OLDHAM STREET CHAPEL, MANCHESTER.

Figure 39. Permission to build the Chapel extensions ©ESRO

It is noted that the Chapel turnover was £69 19s 0d in 1874 but only £21 5s 2d in 1898, which would suggest a significant fall in activity. Also in 1893 a proposal was made to reduce the Chapel debt with money raised being sent directly to the Trustees to reduce this.

The chapel was not recognised for solemnizing marriages until 1898 when there is an entry in the London Gazette of 16 August 1898:

'NOTICE is hereby given that a separate building named Wesleyan Chapel situated at Station-road, Battle in the civil parish of Battle in the county of

Sussex in the registration district of Battle being a building certified according to law as a place of meeting for religious worship, was on 8th day of August 1898, duly registered for solemnizing marriages therein, pursuant to the Act of 6th and 7th Wm. 4, c.85.'

Peter Coote of the present Methodist Church has spent some considerable time looking at the records that he could find from 1903 onwards and his notes are incorporated in the next few pages.

The building was originally called the Wesleyan Chapel as is clear from old photographs, but in more recent years it has been known as Battle Methodist Church. By 1903 the chapel had been up for 77 years. A look at the Minute books shows that from the beginning there was a great deal of work needed in maintenance of this old building.

There was a good Sunday School before WW1(Fig.40), but this disappeared between the World Wars for various reasons. Strangely this did not re-start for many years until Peter Coote arrived in 1981. He then handed it on to Alastair Munro in 1988, who in turn handed over to Ann Menzies in 2004. She had previously assisted both Messrs. Coote and Munro and she runs it to the present day.

Fortunately, there were always good people able and willing to share the responsibilities with each other. Some were Trustees or Stewards; others played the organ for services or arranged flowers to beautify the chapel for the same services. Still others cared for the finances or kept records of meetings; while others had different abilities in building or decorating. But, as now, it was an uphill struggle.

There were so many men and women taking an energetic care of the fabric of the chapel in the early 20th century that it would be unfair to single out some names and not others, but certain people stand out in the dry words of the minutes.

For example, there was one Mr. F. Jempson. He first appears in 1914 and then reappears, year after year in various responsibilities, viz. steward, sides-man, carrier out of all sorts of decorating jobs, repairs etc. He had a business at 40, High Street, of builder and decorator and so was able to do things the others would only have the slightest idea how to do. He last appears in 1952. Then he just disappears from the scene, without any mention. I wonder what happened?

Figure 40. The Methodist Sunday School circa.1911

In 1903 there is mention of one Mr. G. Cramp who was conductor of the choir and a steward and then in 1921 he became the trust secretary, a job he kept till 1936. Then there was a Mr. E. Truman who held the task of Steward for over 8 years.

Early trustees had special responsibilities. They were personally supposed to care for the fabric of the chapel and did so most faithfully until an Act of Parliament[64] approved the modern Methodist Church and a Model Deed under which every member of the church was to share this task.

Before Church Councils came into being in 1974 and became the 'managing trustees' there were Leaders' Meetings which dealt with spiritual and pastoral matters and Trustees' Meetings which dealt with the fabric. In addition the trustees held an annual meeting with a minister in the chair for full discussion of everything pertaining to the building and there were Quarterly Leaders' Meetings chaired by the minister for everything else. Trustees were voted into office for life even if he or she moved to another part of the country.

It is noticeable that Mr. F. Jempson is never mentioned as one of the trustees. It is possible that he felt it could be misunderstood if one of

---

64 Methodist Church Union Act 1929

the trustees always got the jobs for repairs, renovations etc. and so, he stayed as a Steward and attended, by invitation the Trustees' Meetings to give his expert opinion as to the best way to go about such jobs. He knew where to get the best materials, at the best price, and, if he had stated a job would be finished by a certain date, it always was most reliably done.

Many different organs have been used down the years and many good people able and willing, have been found to play the accompaniments. Among such musicians must be mentioned the Misses Young in 1903, Mrs. Jempson in 1920, Mr. Crump in 1922 and perhaps most of all Miss M. Crump in 1923 to 1948, whose place was taken by Mrs. C. Freeland until 1961 when it was taken over by Mrs. Mabel Day (actually this was Miss M. Crump again), who continued to the late 1980's. She had been part of the music for 70 years and had been so recognized by the Methodist Music Society. That's an extraordinary record unlikely to be broken soon.

The old rather daunting pulpit (Fig.41) was removed in 1954 to make way for more modern church furniture.

Figure 41. The old pulpit

There must have been organs with the bellows operated by foot-pedals over the years, but I can find no mention of what they were until 1961, when it was stated that 'a new organ was to be purchased for £287 and the floor made good under it' I believe this was a 'Selmers' instrument. Then a Hammond organ was bought for £250 "A bargain not to be missed" said Mr. Foster of Rye. This was still in use when I arrived at Battle in 1981. In about 1999 we bought the present "Eminent" digital organ for many thousands of pounds. The old trustees would have been shocked at this.

A new set of iron railings and gates were installed in 1950 in memory of Elizabeth Freeman. In photographs of 1911 the Chapel had a wicket fence and gate but there is a note relating to the 1950 installation saying that these replaced those requisitioned during WW2. So there must have been a previous set of metal railings after 1911.

A small kitchen and toilet block was added to the rear south west side of the church in the 1970s before English Heritage listing would have made such changes very difficult.

From this point forwards the church was requiring more and more maintenance and upgrading e.g. new windows and doors, work to walls to waterproof them and a new damp course. All of this resulted in spiralling fabric costs. These were offset greatly by a church working group, started by Harry Lane and including stalwarts such as Eric Diss, Harold Durrant, Leslie Ball and Tony Day, who worked tirelessly to maintain the church during the 1980s and 1990s (Fig.42). But as they got older this became more difficult. By 2000 it was estimated by Eric Diss that about £50,000 overall had been paid on this work to contractors and for materials but that the labour costs saved by the working group had been about £40,000, both over a 20 year period. This was a superb service to the chapel. The small gallery (Fig.43) was removed for safety reasons in 1990.

By 2002 it was necessary to undertake a major refurbishment to the kitchen and WC. This triggered a recognition that the continuing rate of expenditure was untenable and early discussions are minuted about the future. In 2004 the Rev. Pen Wilcock openly voiced her doubts about the long term viability of continuing with the chapel as it was. After this another £6000 was spent on repairs in the next two or three years. In 2007 a special Church Council was held to consider a report from the Rev. David Freeland, and the decision was taken by the Council to vacate the old 1826 Grade II listed building and move to a new building. This decision was also influenced by the Council's vision of having a Church which was easily accessible and multi-purpose, for use of the community 7 days a week and not just on Sundays.

Figure 42. The Church interior in 2011. Bright and welcoming the new décor was the work of the Church Working Group.

Figure 43. The Methodist Church Balcony before demolition.
Photo 22/11/89 by the late Harold Durrant

Given the size of the congregation (around 50) this may have seemed ambitious, but the members set up four groups to take this decision forwards, co-ordinated by Alastair Munro. These groups were to:

1. Sell the existing Chapel ;
2. Find a new location;
3. Design the building;
4. Raise the funds to build it

The membership of these groups changed over time but those who have contributed through the majority of the project to date have been: Merle Bailey, Dana Budd, Beryl Finbow, Fitz Fitzgraham, Keith Foord, Paula Foord, Christine Freeland, David Freeland, Andrew Knowles-Baker, Alastair Munro and Jane Munro.

It took time to get some momentum and direction, but by August 2008 a 0.4 hectare (just under one acre) site at 'Blackfriars' off Harrier Lane, Battle had been identified and Rother District Council who own this community land agreed in principle to sell it to the Church.

The land is part of a one hectare area zoned for community use. From the outset it had been agreed that the new building would be multi-purpose and serve its local community with availability of access for multiple purposes seven days a week.

In April 2009 outline planning permission was applied for but it was refused as Rother District Council considered that the land should not be built on until a comprehensive plan for developing the whole one hectare site was available. However there was no indication that such a plan would be forthcoming at any time in the immediate future and the working group therefore decided to appeal this decision, making clear that there would be full co-operation in the future concerning access and development of the upper part of the one hectare site. In March 2010 the National Planning Inspectorate upheld this appeal.

Consultation was held to determine what local people wanted from the facility. Questionnaires were circulated and door to door calls were made and a meeting held with Battle Town Council. This confirmed that there was indeed likely to be demand for the meeting rooms and open spaces planned for the building.

In May 2010 Rother District Council formally agreed to sell the 0.4 hectare to Battle Methodist Church and after an informal competition Pinelog Ltd. of Bakewell, Derbyshire were selected to provide architectural and building services on a 'Design and Build' basis.

One concern about the 'Blackfriars' site was there might be an area of landfill at the boundary of the site with Harrier Lane and therefore the risk of environmental pollution. In March 2011 a full environmental survey gave the 'all clear' establishing that there were no landfill or pollution or other concerns.

In May 2011 the existing 1826 Chapel was advertised for sale and an offer accepted. It is expected that by September/October of 2011 both the sale and purchases will have been finalised and the detailed design agreed between Battle Methodist Church and Pinelog.

The next point is not without some pain to members as the old Chapel will be vacated on completion of the contracts. Obviously all are sad to be leaving the old Chapel with its history and many memories, but they look forward with anticipation to an interesting future.

After that detailed/full planning permission will be requested and a formal contract signed with Pinelog Ltd. At the time of writing (August 2011) it is expected that this will be before Christmas 2011.

If all goes well site clearance and preparation will start by March 2012, with final handover of the new Church and Community building in late 2012.

This will be much looked forward to as between October 2011 and late 2012 it has been agreed that the Church will meet for Sunday Services in the function room at the back of the Senlac Inn, just opposite the old Chapel. It is believed that it is not the first time that Methodist meetings have been held on pub premises, but of course only teas and coffees and soft drinks will be available in the temporary housing!

The working ideas, designs and site plan are covered in Chapter 15 – The Future

Methodist Ministers involved at Battle

The author has been able to identify many but not all of the ministers appointed to the Hastings Circuit who have been involved with Battle. The list, in spite of its incompleteness particularly for the 1800s, is long as it was normal for ministers to stay in the circuit only 3 years (though it is now usually longer) and to cover more than one church.

1804	Rev. J Bagnall	
1875	Rev. C O Eldridge	
1902	Rev. L J Nicholson	
1907	Rev. B Norton	
1908	Rev. J Mathewman	
1910	Rev C Wenyon	
1911	Rev. H G Godwin / Rev. G Gregor / Rev. A	Summerfield
1914	Rev F Chur	
1916	Rev. H M Draper / Rev. J G Radford	
1922	Rev T W Fawthrop	

1923	Rev. W W Vicary
1928	Rev. Percy Mellor
1929	Rev. E Shell Richards
1931	Rev. J W Hallam
1934	Rev. Thomas H Sheriff
1935	Rev. J J Johnson
1940	Rev. A B Duncalfe
1946	Rev. C A Somerscales
1949	Rev. G H B Sketchley
1951	Rev. G Arnold Wise
1952	Rev. A C Stanisland
1956	Rev. Harold C Hubbard
1960	Rev. L Lazenby
1963	Rev. G Poole
1966	Rev. H Allen
1971	Rev. E Harrup
1973	Rev. David Freeland*
1975	Rev. Irving Penberthy
1980	Rev. Alan Warrell
1984	Rev. Frank May
1990	Rev. Tom Holcombe (an American)
1992	Rev. Arnold Stacey
1995	Rev. Richard Chapple
1996	Rev. Alan Hewitt
2001	Rev. Roy Smith
2003	Rev. Penelope Wilcock
2006	Rev. David Freeland*
2007	Rev. Marion Proud
2011	Rev. Peggy Heim (another American)

The same person

The Circuits

Most branches of Methodism have four levels of government: the national Conference; the District (a regional grouping); the Circuit (a local grouping of congregations); and the Society. The last two levels only are represented by locally held records.

The Society consists of the formal membership of an individual chapel; others may attend, but are not members. Not all Societies had actual buildings, and preaching meetings, some open-air, could be held in places where there was no Society. Within the Societies, Leaders ran Classes (groups) of members and Trusts were concerned with buildings and manses as well as chapels and churches.

Circuits tended to be large in earlier years, splitting up as membership increased. In recent years the trend has been reversed, with Circuits amalgamating into much larger units again. The Circuit usually represents an area grouping of Societies, though occasionally a Society was a Circuit in itself. Ministers are generally appointed to Circuits, with the senior minister as Superintendent, and are fewer in number than the meeting places; much use is made of lay preachers.

Hastings Circuit was formed in 1822 and consisted of chapels at Hastings, Bexhill, Westfield, Battle, Hooe and Guestling. During the next few years chapels at Eastbourne, Waldron, Hellingly, Sedlescombe, Ninfield, Hollington, Catsfield, Crowhurst, Pevensey Sluice, Netherfield and Fairlight were added though the first three were transferred to Lewes circuit in 1825.

By 1843 chapels at St. Leonards, Catsfield, Little Common and Netherfield had been added and by 1860 a chapel at Ashburnham.

In 1886 the circuit was divided and Norman Road, New Park Road and Caves Road in St Leonards, Belle Hill and Little Common in Bexhill, Ninfield and Dallington formed a new St. Leonards circuit .

Guestling joined the Hastings circuit in 1894 and remained till 1914, coming back again in 1934. Westfield and Icklesham were added in 1934, and Pett in 1937.

In 1966, to the existing Hastings Circuit consisting of Central, Wesley Mission and Calvert Memorial in Hastings, Hollington, Ore, Catsfield, Crowhurst, Mountfield, Westfield, Guestling, Icklesham and Pett were added Rye, Winchelsea, Beckley, Peasmarsh, Iden and Wittersham (Kent) from the Rye Circuit.

In due course the Hastings and St Leonards Circuits merged into the existing Hastings, Bexhill and Rye Circuit.

Chapter 9

Dissenters 1813 until sometime after 1835

In common with the maelstrom of radical protestantism occurring all over Britain multiple other small dissenting groups were to be founded in Battle in the 19th century.

It is perhaps difficult for us to appreciate the importance of religion in the lives of people who lived in the Eighteenth and Nineteenth centuries, as we live in a secular world where material things seem to have more importance than things spiritual. Small differences in interpretation of the Bible led individuals to question even newly established Non-conformist churches and a few set up their own house churches.

Unfortunately no records can be found other than their registrations for worship by the Diocese of Chichester[65]. These are listed below in date order. Those who can be traced at WSRO are in **bold**, the others in *bold italic* have come from the 'On-line parish clerks' website.

1813: Dissenters. At a house in Whatlington and another in *1820:* On the High Street of Battle.

28 June 1820: Congregation of Protestant Dissenters in a dwelling house in Netherfield in Battle parish in occupation of Thomas Coleman.

15 April 1826: Congregation of Protestants in a dwelling house in Darvelhole, Battle, in occupation of Joseph Catt[66]
1829: Free Thinking Christians (? where)

23 January 1835: Congregation of Protestant Dissenters in the dwelling house of Daniel Macpherson near the Watch Oak, Battle.
No Daniel Macpherson living in Battle can be found in the census of

---

65 WSRO Ep II/25/3
66 These were probably Wesleyans

1841. It is clearly not a local name and in fact only two Daniel Macphersons were recorded in England in the 1841 censuses – in Durham and Northumberland. It may be that Daniel Macpherson was somehow attached to the militia based at Battle Barracks.

23 January 1835: Congregation of Protestant Dissenters in a dwelling house in the occupation of William Bones and others in that part of Battle known as The Hill.

A William Bones became a Trustee of the Zion Baptist Church on 30 Sep 1857, having joined the church in 1851[67]. To confuse matters no less than six William Bones can be identified in or near Battle in the 1841 census.

1. William Bones (aged 33) lived with Alfred (27, ?his brother) and Dina Bones (69, ? his mother) and James Freeman (59, ? a lodger) at Whatlington Mill.
2. William Bones (aged 50) lived with his wife and family including a son William (aged 11) at Battle Hill.
3. William Bones (aged 60) lived with his wife and family including a son William (aged 20) on Hastings Road, Battle. This family had an 'insane' daughter Harriet.
4. William Bones (aged 40) lodged with the Isted family at Reeves, Ashburnham.

The William Bones Senior of Battle Hill is the most likely person to have been the registrant of the Congregation of Protestant Dissenters in a dwelling house in that part of Battle known as The Hill in 1835.

---

67 History of Battle Baptist Church

Chapter 10
Strict Baptists 1870 – about 1920

Strict Baptists met in a rented upper room of the Langton Hall (Fig.44) from 1870-1920. They would have almost certainly been a breakaway group from the Particular Baptists of Zion Chapel, possibly because by 1873 the practice of admitting unbaptised believers to the membership was made lawful by a new rule of the Zion Baptist Chapel.

Figure 44. Langton Hall from Abbey Green in early 1900s

Joseph Newbery was a leading member of this group and opened the chapel. Joseph was a senior member of the Newbery family who started a local factory in the latter part of the 19th century with his brother George to make preserves including canned goods, jam, boiled sweets and jellies. This had evolved from his father Henry's bakery. Joseph and his wife, Kezia from West Meon in Hampshire, had at least 11 children.

Regular services were held on Sundays, morning and evening. There was no regular preacher and so the services were conducted by

ministers of the sect from neighbouring areas. No musical instruments were permitted except on rare occasions, but a single note from a flute or pitch pipe was used to start the first verse of each hymn[68]
Although they never had their own building they may have used the Congregational chapel some time later. Joseph and Kezia Newbery's oldest daughter, Rose Bertha (Rosie), married in the Congregational church in 1909. Sadly a son Charles Joseph was killed in Flanders in 1915 during WWI .

The following information is drawn from the Strict Baptist's History website[69]:

Strict Baptists had emerged as a distinct body early in the 19th century, because of their belief in a strict Calvinist interpretation of the doctrine of salvation.
Many evangelical Churches invite 'all who love the Lord Jesus Christ' to take the bread and wine at the Lord's Table. Strict Baptists, like many other groups of Baptist Churches elsewhere in the world, believe that this privilege should be offered only to those who have been baptised by immersion as believers.
For Strict Baptists restricting communion in this way does not imply that those who are not admitted are not Christians; it follows solely from Strict Baptist beliefs about the Church, Baptism and the Lord's Supper.
Strict Baptists see Baptism as a rite by which believers testify to their faith in Christ, and associate it with church membership. Strict Baptists believe that the Lord's Supper is only for those who have joined the church in this way. The term Strict therefore refers to this practice of 'restricted communion'.

---

68   B. Newberry recorded in L. Boys-Behrens book, Battle Abbey under 39 Kings
69   http://www.strictbaptisthistory.org.uk/

Chapter 11
The Church of the Ascension, Telham
1876 – 2011

This Church lies at 128m (420 feet) above sea level at nearly the highest point on the sandstone Battle Ridge extension of the High Weald of Sussex, which extends towards Hastings and ends at Fairlight cliffs and the cliffs at Hastings itself.

Telham Hill, just west of the Church, north of the road to Crowhurst, is probably the site at which William mustered his forces before the Battle of Hastings. As William had been encamped at Hastings before the battle the choice of Telham as a mustering site would have been logical. However we now jump forwards 911 years.

From some time before 1877 up to the time this chapel was opened services at Telham had been conducted in 'Mr Turley's barn', opposite the turning to Crowhurst from the Battle-Hastings road.

Initially named "Mission Chapel of the Ascension" this church (Figs. 45 and 47) stands on 828 sq m (32 3/4 rods) of land given to Dean Edward Crake of Battle in 1875 by Sir Archibald Lamb, who owned the large Beauport Estate which stretched towards Battle from the outskirts of Hastings. He had originally offered another site in 1874, possibly nearer the Black Horse pub, but this was deemed unsuitable. Before the church was built Dean Crake had referred to the site as the 'Black Horse Chapel site'.

The building was constructed during 1876 on behalf of and paid for by the then Dean of Battle, the Very Reverend Dr. Edward Neville Crake (Fig.46). To confirm this a stone under the altar window bears the date 1876.

The original intention of Dean Crake was that the building should be used as a school during the week and a mission chapel on Sundays and for other purposes 'in connection with the Church of England'.

It was initially not to be consecrated. However it was given a discretionary licence for use as a place of worship by the Bishop of Chichester in 1877, for the benefit of Battle residents, living at a distance from the Parish Church. This obviously was to replace Mr Turley's barn, but was undoubtedly also to some degree a response to the inroads the Non-conformists of Battle had made on the numbers of worshippers in the Church of England. A further dedication was made on 29th April 1880.

In his will of 1909 Dean Crake left his house on Abbey Green the proceeds of which were to be kept in a Trust to be used for the upkeep of the Telham church. Its sale realised £343 8s 4d and this money plus another £15 3s 9d was originally invested in India 3 1/2% Stocks and initially produced £15 per annum. After the passing of the Trustee Investment Act, 1961 the endowment was changed to 468.62 COIF Charity fund shares and produced a little more. The COIF Fund originated from the Charities Deposit Fund that was formed in 1985 as a Common Deposit Fund for charities.

Figure 45. SE view of the Church of the Ascension, Telham

The income from the fund is administered in conformity with the Charity Commissioners scheme of 4 June 1912 under the title of 'Dean Crake's gift' A trust deed was drawn up by the Charity Commission, which covers the fabric of the building and its maintenance and also allows for the building's use as *'a Chapel, school for the education of poor persons, as a residence for a schoolmaster or schoolmistress, for literary, scientific or musical entertainment or for use for meetings or other uses connected with the parish work of the Dean and his Curates'.* The trustees of this are the current Dean of Battle and Churchwardens. In practice they are joined by six members of the congregation appointed annually at an AGM. Fund raising is ongoing, on behalf of the trust, in order to maintain the Church and Churchyard and a number of smallish legacies have been received.

Figure 46. The Very Reverend Dr. Edward Neville Crake

The church is of red brick with a tiled roof. There is a small belfry towards its east end with a fixed bell with another small belfry attached to the west wall containing three tubular bells given in memory of Gertrude Breeds (d.1911)(Fig.47).

A wooden eagle lectern is a memorial to Margaret Christie (d.1892) and the east window to the Rev. Campbell Manning Christie, who served the church from its beginning until his death in 1880. At the time of repairs to this window in 1989 it was suggested that this window may have originally been that of another church, but there is no record of this.

A small portable organ was given to the church in about 1898 by a Miss Duke of Telham Lane, but by 1970 needed replacement. So in 1970 a second hand Norvic type B organ was purchased from the church of St Margaret at Fenhurst for £35, installed at Telham at a total cost of £370 and dedicated on Saturday 10th October 1970 by the

V. Rev. H R Darby. It was then overhauled in 1999 at a further cost of £5934 and re-dedicated on Sunday 28th November 1999 by the V. Rev William A V Cummings. A new altar frontal was dedicated at Easter 1995.

It is believed that there was a Sunday School at one time, but the only record of this is for a girl named Kate St. Clair Conquer for whom a baptism certificate survives dated 20th January 1907 plus four more certificates which date through to Christmas 1915. It is also believed that at one time there was a choir but no written or photographic evidence of this exists.

Figure 47. The Church showing its two belfries

The church has unfortunately been the scene of a number of burglaries and also impact damage from traffic incidents. Significant damage was done to the building on 11th January 1996 by a vehicle followed by associated fire and smoke damage, which cost £12,000 to rectify.

Another incident happened on 19th June 1997 when the iron railings were substantially damaged. The railings have been replaced by special safety fencing and East Sussex County Council have now painted double white lines and erected bend warning signs.

To mark the year 2000 a yew tree propagated in that year from the Tandridge Yew, Surrey which is estimated to be about 2500 years old, was presented to the church by Prof. David Bellamy OBE, President of the Conservation Foundation. This was planted to the rear of the church on Mothering Sunday 25th March 2001 by Canon David Fricker.

The history of the donor (Sir Archibald Lamb, of Beauport Park) of the land on which the church was built is also of historical interest. The first mention of Beauport Park is when General Sir James Murray is shown in local records as paying rates on some woodland. He built the house between 1763 and 1766, subsequently added to the estate until it comprised about 20 km^2 (5,000 acres). Murray had served under General James Wolfe at the Battle of the Plains of Abraham in 1759. He was the military commander of Quebec City after it fell to the British and he named the local estate after Beauport in Canada. Following Murray's death in 1794, Beauport Park was purchased by James Bland Burgess who served as Under Secretary of State for Foreign Affairs to William Pitt. In 1821, James and his eldest son Charles changed their name to Lamb in honour of John Lamb, a benefactor of theirs. James became a Baronet in 1795.....

By 1860, the estate was owned by Sir Charles Lamb's son, Archibald, who leased the house to Thomas Brassey, a leading railway engineer of his day. After Thomas Brassey died in 1870 the lease was inherited by his son who later became Lord Brassey who lived at Normanhurst.

Archibald Lamb's father, also Charles, died before his own father and on his grandfather's death in 1860 Archibald became the 3rd Baronet, in addition to inheriting yet another 11 km^2 (2700 acres) of land. So he would have hardly noticed the loss of the small parcel of land by the main Hastings to Battle road that he gave to Dean Crake in 1875.

A significant amount of information about this Church has been supplied from a leaflet by Alec B. Carter written in 2001 given to the author by Julia Thorp. He in turn acknowledged the help he had been given by the late Brig. Sam Learmont, who had given him some information about Telham and also the late Harry Cockcroft who was organist at the Church for more than 42 years before he retired in April 1973. Harry lived to be 100 on 10th July 1991 dying the following November.

Chapter 12
Congregationalists 1881 – 1950?

Figure 48. The old Congregational Chapel, Battle High Street

The original Congregational churches were formed based on a theory published by the theologian Robert Browne in 1592 and developed from the Non-conformist religious movement in England during the Puritanical reformation.

By 1850 Congregationalism had been transformed from a string of meeting houses all with a commitment to the complete autonomy of the local congregation into a network of thriving chapels placed prominently on main streets. The idea that each congregation fully constituted the local Church can be traced to John Wycliffe and the Lollard movement, which followed after Wycliffe was removed from teaching authority in the Roman Catholic Church.

In 1850 there were over 3,200 Congregational churches. But a national Congregational church may be seen as a contradiction in terms, the very nature of Congregationalism being that the local

124

church is independent of all other churches in its work and administration. Congregationalism is a "grass roots" movement .

So Battle Congregational Chapel and Sunday School (Fig.48) was a late arrival when it opened on the High Street on 28 July 1881. It can still be seen today as an architectural anomaly, as it is set back from the line of the shop fronts. Its façade is built in weathered red brick with a cream stone porch, with two steps up from the recessed pavement and with two large windows to each side of the porch and a smaller one over it, all headed with the same cream stone. To the rear it has zero architectural merit (the modern equivalent would be a steel box warehouse), but nevertheless it is Grade II listed by English Heritage, presumably for its façade.

The Congregational Chapel was founded in Battle by a group of 22 persons who had left the Zion Chapel when they re-instated adult baptism by total immersion in 1880. They obviously considered that their previous infant baptism should have sufficed. Prominent amongst these was Jonathan Jenner who had been a Baptist lay-preacher as well as the Baptist Chapel's treasurer and deacon. He was a local farmer[70] who had been born in 1823, married Mary Pursglove and had eight children. The group funded the building of a new Chapel 14m x 6m (46 ft by 20 ft) with a rear room of 5.6m x 4.9m (18 ft 6 in x 16 ft) on High Street, Battle. Later they joined the Sussex Congregational Union.

Its architect was Thomas W Elworthy who also built at least three other churches locally – St Leonards Baptist Church, Chapel Park Road, St Leonards on Sea in 1883, Robertsbridge Congregational Church (now United Reformed Church), 1881 and a church at Hughenden Place, Hastings in 1878 (demolished 1972). The first two show distinct similarities to the Battle High Street church. It may be that the architect used a pattern book. One wonders why it appears so anonymous. It almost hides itself away. Maybe it appears so self effacing as Battle High Street is such a busy shopping area with all the shop fronts on the same building line .... and it is so obviously not a shop and not in line.

In 1891 delegates from this church to the Eastern District meetings

70 He farmed at Little Park Farm, having left the family farm at Boreham Street.

were W C Jenner[71] and R B Allwork, but after that only the occasional minister is noted at these meetings. In 1901 the church contributed £5 19s 0d to District funds. The only other event that is recorded (as a by product of a genealogy site) is that Rosie Newbery of the local Newbery family of preserves, jam and sweets fame who were Strict Baptists married in this church in 1909.

From 7 September 1923 it was regulated by a Charity Commissioners scheme, with the Sussex Congregational Union being the trustees. Its last services look as if they were held in 1949 or 1950 just after the Second World War during which the Baptist Pastor had held services on alternate weeks between his own church and the Congregational Church.

For many years it stood empty and, when asked, few seemed to know what it had been. It was finally sold in 1976 and was bought by the Jenner family for use as a storeroom and they also put in an upper floor to make some offices. They sold it on in the early 1990s as part of the Jenner Mill site re-development, but obviously it cannot be changed much as the building is now Grade II listed. In recent years it has been used as a delicatessen, offices and several different restaurants.

Its list of ministers can be found from the Surman index[72]

1882-1888	Chapple, George Porter
1889-1893	Morgan, John
1893-1897	Nicholson, William
1897-1901	Dakin, David Samuel
1902-1906	Eldridge, William James,
1906-1914	Roberts, William John
?	
Abt 1928- 1931?	Weller, Thomas Cyril
1931-1933	Martin, Henry
?	
1936-1940	Heming, Clarence William Wesley

71 William Caleb Jenner was Jonathan Jenner's second son
72 The Surman Index Online, Dr Williams's Centre for Dissenting Studies, http://surman.english.qmul.ac.uk

?

| 1942-1946 | *Cover by Baptist minister* |
| 1947-1949 | Hooker, John Mitchell |

As early as the late 1800s some Congregationalists had been alarmed at the diminution in their membership. They had called for union with another denomination to increase the size and effectiveness of the churches.

At one stage, some consideration was given to the idea that the Baptist Union and the Congregational Union might unite. A joint assembly of these two bodies was held in 1901. Even though the only real difference between the Baptists and Congregationalists was on the issue of baptism, many Congregationalists preferred to look to the Presbyterians for union. Eventually talks with the Presbyterians were held after the second world war but came to nothing. In the meanwhile at a local level things had got closer as in 1906 there was serious consideration given to merging.

Clearly the numbers of Congregationalists in Battle waned to nearly zero post WW2 and the church was closed. It remains unclear as to exactly when but in 1948 the Battle Congregational Church was still receiving monies from The Congregationalist's Sussex Eastern District and the last recorded mention of Battle in their minutes was in 1950 - when it was considered that Battle should be included with Robertsbridge. After that there is no note.

In the late 20th century English Presbyterians, English, Welsh and Scottish Congregationalists and members of the Churches of Christ eventually amalgamated through a series of unions in 1972, 1981 and 2000 to become the United Reformed Church, but far too late for Battle. It can be noted however that the Robertsbridge United Reformed Church is still going strong with weekly services.

If it looks vaguely familiar it is because the Battle and Robertsbridge churches had the same architect who seemed to have that pattern book.....Pevsner (or more likely Iain Nairn) is recorded as not liking it.

Chapter 13

Catholics after 1538 and the Catholic Church of Our Lady Immaculate and Saint Michael 1882(7) – 2011

Figure 49. The front of the Roman Catholic Church with Florence Cottages to the left

After the reformation Catholicism was replaced by the Church of England as the religion of England. It could for a time be dangerous to be a practising Catholic, but some of the nobility somehow retained their positions, notably the Dukes of Norfolk. The surprise as far as Battle is concerned is to find that the descendants of Sir Anthony Browne, the new lord of the manor, retained their Catholicism.

Sir Anthony's son, also Anthony, undertook an embassy to Rome soon after the accession of Queen Mary I to restore the authority of the Pope in England and was made Viscount Montagu for these services at the time of the marriage of Mary with Philip of Spain. He promptly left the Privy Council on the death of Mary I and the accession of Queen Elizabeth I.

This episode is described as follows in the Collected charters etc. of Battle Abbey:

"Anthony, the son, was one of the forty Knights created at the Coronation of King Edward VI. For the more honourable reception of Philip of Spain, then about to be married to Mary I, was appointed, on April 8, 1554, Master of the Horse to that King; and on Sept. 2 following, by letters patent, advanced to the dignity of Viscount Montagu, which title he chose, by reason that the Lady Lucy, his grandmother, was one of the daughters and co-heirs to John Nevil, Marquis Montagu.

He was then deputed, by order of Parliament, together with Thomas Thurlby, Bishop of Ely, to the Pope, to render the submission of these realms to an accordance and union with the Church of Rome, and to the obedience of that see.

He was afterwards of the Queen's Privy Council, and consulted in most affairs during her turbulent and mischievous reign. The accession of Elizabeth diffused a gleam of brightness more consonant to the feelings of the nation and the Viscount, known as a staunch Romanist, was omitted in the selection of the members of the Privy Council." ....

"In the second year of Elizabeth I's reign, in the grand debate in Parliament for the annulling of the Pope's supremacy and restoring it to the Crown of England only he and the Earl of Shrewsbury voted against that abolition."

But this did not stop him still being a useful person to the Crown as in the next year the following occurred.

" Notwithstanding his devotion to the Romish faith, his prudence and wisdom evinced him a loyal and dutiful subject, and he was considered, in the ensuing year, as the most acceptable person to be sent as ambassador from England to Philip the Second of Spain, to satisfy him of the just causes the Queen had to send an armed force into Scotland, and to represent that

the practices of the Guises[73] might be of as dangerous consequences to his provinces in the Netherlands, as well as in Spain, as they were to England." The Viscount was also one of the Peers who presided on the trial of Mary Queen of Scots. Elizabeth I obviously appreciated his continuing services and paid him a visit some short time before his death, at Horsley, in Surrey, on 19th October 1592.

In 1596 Lady Montague is recorded as having a resident priest and a schoolmaster at Battle Abbey manor house who are supposed to have been on friendly terms with the Dean of Battle who was said to be 'very lax in performing his liturgical functions'. Lady Montague died in 1608 and her biographer, Richard Smith (1627) says that she built a chapel and attracted large congregations for the Catholic services.

Through the early years of the 17th century no fewer than three priests were resident in Battle ; Thomas More, Thomas Smith and the above Richard Smith (1603-09). The last became the second Vicar Apostolic[74] of England in 1625. Also near Battle were other recusant families such as the Pelhams of Catsfield and the Ashburnhams.

But overall the Catholic population of Battle shrank in the 17th century mainly it is supposed because the Montagues preferred from the early 17th century to live and worship at Cowdray House rather than Battle. In lists made in 1717 and 1723 only five local Catholics are named – James Ashenden, Nicholas Eldridge, Mary Brewer and Chrisogonus Manhood of Battle and Henry Martin of Sedlescombe, all of whom held land but were taxed for their religion. In 1742 and 1748 Bishop Challener of London held visitations at Battle and in 1758 a report mentions 'Mr Bennett, a Popish priest' living at Battle. By 1767 there were 16 Catholics in Battle and 5 at Sedlescombe.

So Catholicism lingered on, but many of its centres became extinct – Battle was the sole survivor in East Sussex and from the late 18th

---

73 The first Duke of Guise (1496–1550), had been made a Duke by King Francis I of France. His daughter, Mary of Guise (1515–1560), married King James V of Scotland and was mother of Mary, Queen of Scots. The Guises were a powerful Catholic family and provoked religious wars against Protestants in France

74 Richard Smith was appointed Catholic Bishop over the whole of England, Wales and Scotland in 1625. In 1628 a warrant was issued for his arrest. He resigned his post in 1631, when he fled to Paris.

century there was a small revival.

The entire initiative for the establishment of a permanent presence in Battle came from Bertram, 5th Earl of Ashburnham, who converted to Catholicism in 1872 at the age of 32. This was a matter of convenience for him – to have a priest nearby rather than have to travel to Hastings. Twice in 1879 he wrote to Bishop Danell of Southwark suggesting 'establishing a mission in the district'. The second time around the Bishop replied approving the suggestion but left the details to the Earl......

A large mission in St Leonards was at the time served by Rev. John Foy. He was naturally concerned to lose his wealthiest parishioner. He told the Earl that there were no Catholics in Battle and he arranged to go himself to Ashburnham Place to say masses. This went on for several years but the Earl still spent some time planning for a parish in Battle.

The Catholic Directory gives the date of the formation of the Battle Mission as 1882, but it was not until 1885 that tenders were sought for a 'new school chapel' to be built at the rear of a garden of a house in Mount Street (now 'The Hollies' formerly Richard Sinnock's house[75]. Fig. 31) which was bought by Lord Ashburnham. This suggests that he bought the house in 1882. The idea was that the chapel should be erected to serve a future school and to be a temporary public church. But first a priest had to be found and the Benedictines of Downside Abbey near Bath were approached. The monks were reluctant and it was not until 1887 that the first priest, Fr Michael Gorman, arrived. He almost immediately started up the school that had been Earl Ashburnham's main purpose.

To do so he used rooms in The Hollies as well as converting other rooms for a second priest (Fr Henry Cafferata), a housekeeper and a temporary chapel. No wonder Fr Cafferatta left only 11 months later complaining of overcrowding.

His first congregation (on 6th November 1887) in The Hollies, consisted of himself and a local banker's wife. He reported that the only other Catholic he could find was a lapsed one who had become an Anglican and Freemason after an argument with a priest two years previously.

---

75   See page 75

But several people had asked when the new church being built behind the house (Figs.49 and 50) would be opened. This happened on 2nd February 1888. It should be noted that at this time the Zion Particular Baptists had only just (in 1886) sold their old wooden meeting house and its land which abutted the new church. In 1897 Florence Cottages were built there and have a common wall with the church, an unusual arrangement which is unexplained.

After his first year Fr Gorman had 10 Catholics to serve, in the next 21 with the numbers including those at Ashburnham House. But Fr Gorman seems to have become unsettled and left in 1892 having twice served as a chaplain on troopships to India earlier that year. His work was covered by Fr Rosette, Rector of St Stanislaus College at Hollington, who arranged for Jesuit priests to cover the church, but Ashburnham was covered from a new Salesian College at Burwash. This continued until a new priest Fr Charles Kimpe arrived in July 1893. He stayed until 1899 when the Salesians covered Ashburnham again whilst Battle had a temporary priest Fr Thomas Mahon, until Fr Joseph Wilhelms arrived in 1900.

For the work of both the school and the presbytery the Hollies was too small. The Earl tried to buy 13 Mount Street but the owner would not sell. The school was big enough for a new house to be built for it in 1902. This was St. Michael's on Caldbec Hill, but the school then failed during WW1 and became an over-large presbytery, with The Hollies being rented out to tenants. The situation reversed in 1924 with The Hollies becoming the presbytery again and St Michaels rented out. St Michael's was finally sold in the early 2000s, now being the site of a block of flats.

Clearly the situation with Ashburnham was tricky. The Earl had wanted some 25 masses per year and for perpetual masses to be said for himself during his lifetime and after his death. Bishop Butt had refused this in 1887 and the earl had seemed content to endow the Church without any conditions. Following the Earl's death in 1913 some masses were said for his soul and this was continued until at least 1932. The chapel at Ashburnham closed in 1913 as the 6th Earl was an Anglican.

Fr Wilhelms retired back to Germany in 1910, followed by cover from Fr Philip Williams before Rev Peter Ryan came, in turn to be succeeded by Fr Rudolph Bullesbach. His name gave difficulties during WW1 when he was asked by Lady Brassey of Normanhurst to say mass for Catholic officers staying at her house to convalesce and he finally asked Fr John Cronin of Bexhill to cover this duty 'because of my poor name'.

Fr Edmund Miller took over in October 1919 and became the first parish priest when Battle became a canonical parish in 1920, but it was impossible to get the church licensed for marriages until 1928 as insufficient Catholic householders could be found to sign the petition for registration. But Fr Miller worked hard in the surrounding countryside and gradually the parishioners rose to be 125 (the Catholic parish covers much of the eastern part of East Sussex and includes Northiam). He became an honorary Canon in 1930, retiring in 1932 when Fr Edmund Loman arrived.

However Fr Miller had big problems at Ashburnham as Lady Catherine Ashburnham, the unmarried daughter of the 5th Earl, took up residence there in 1924 when the 6th Earl died without a direct male heir. She re-opened the domestic chapel. This was initially served by the Jesuits from Ore Place. Relations with Fr Miller were bad from the start as he considered that since the chapel was in his parish he should have some input and the Sunday collection. Lady Catherine ignored him. She was briefly on good terms with Fr Loman but the dispute broke out again. Various arrangements were made by Lady Catherine to cover masses until her death in 1953 when the chapel was closed for good, but clearly she led a strange and not particularly happy life.

There is a rumour that Lady Catherine's executors offered Ashburnham House to the Bishop of Southwark to buy for a convent (Lady Catherine had tried to get a convent into Battle earlier in 1933, when she had pressed the Ursulines to take over St Michael's on Caldbec Hill). This was impossible as no part of the estate was Lady Catherine's to bequeath and the house and estate passed to a cousin, John Bickersteth, who subsequently took Anglican orders . Seven years after inheriting the estate he gave it to the Ashburnham Christian Trust[76], a registered charity.

---

76 www.ashburnham.org.uk/

After 1953 events at Battle have been more orderly. Fr. Loman retired that year and priests since then have pursued their normal parish duties.

The parish does cover a large area and over time there have been other centres served other than Battle and Ashburnham. These include Whatlington and Robertsbridge both of which have interesting stories outside of the scope of this book.

The Rectors of the Roman Catholic Church of Our Lady Immaculate and Saint Michael

Rev. Michael Gorman	1887-1892
Rev. Charles Kimpe	1893-1899
Rev. Thomas Mahon	1899-1900
Rev. Joseph Wilhelms, DD	1900-1910
Rev. Peter Ryan, DD	1910-1914
Rev. Rudolph Bullesbach	1914-1919
V. Rev. Canon Edmund Miller	1919-1932
Rev. Edmund Loman	1932-1953
Rev. Paul Crommelin	1953-1956
Rev. John Walsh	1956-1959
Rev. Michael Carroll	1959-1978
Father Vincent Maxwell	1978-1987,
Father Terence McLean Wilson	1987-2005,
Father Michael McGlade	2005-2006
Father Anthony White	2006 to date

What has not been described so far is the church itself. The following are some abstracts from the English Heritage Review of Diocesan Churches 2005 : Our Lady Immaculate & St Michael is a modest building of no great architectural importance. The Church was built in 1886, but the architect is not known. The 5th Earl of Ashburnham, founded and paid for the church, but there is a letter to the Roman Catholic Bishop of Southwark from Arnold & Co of 60 Carey Street, Lincoln's Inn, London, 9 January 1886, 'Herewith is list of tenders and the architect will unless we heard (sic) to the contrary from Lord Ashburnham conclude with the lowest. Kindly notice what a difference between the first and the last!'

The present Presbytery is The Hollies, 13 Mount Street, an early 18th century double fronted house clad in white painted weatherboard (listed Grade II). The church is built in what was its garden.

The church is of modest proportions, of dark red brick in an Italianate cum Romanesque style, somewhat unusual for a Catholic church. The west front is gabled and has a central doorway with three windows above, all round arched and with shafts, but also keystones with a broad segmental arch rising from rusticated pilasters. The windows are iron framed. The interior is plastered, with a canted ceiling on corbelled trusses. Three stained glass windows in the nave are by Cox & Barnard of Hove.

Figure 50. The Roman Catholic Church interior

Finally, in view of the importance of the Ashburnhams to the founding of the church here is a brief history of that family.

They emerged as small landowners in the parish of Ashburnham in Sussex towards the close of the twelfth century. They continued there unnoticed for the next four hundred years. But by the time of Queen Elizabeth I the family had become important enough for the heralds to record their pedigree.

It was an Elizabethan Ashburnham, Sir John, knighted at the Tower of London by James I on 14 March 1604[77] who may be credited with starting the family on the road to fame and fortune but he soon lost the money. He was forced to sell the estate and died a debtor in the Fleet Prison in 1620.

His son, a more distinguished John, acquired a position at the court of Charles I through the influence of George Villiers, Duke of Buckingham, a cousin of John Ashburnham's mother, Elizabeth Beaumont. John served Charles I with devotion and is recorded at being present at Charles' execution and suffered long imprisonment and heavy losses in the royal cause. He and his brother William both survived the Commonwealth to see the Restoration of the monarchy and to augment their wealth and prestige.

From that time the Ashburnhams prospered. The cavalier's grandson, another John, was given a Barony by William III, and his son, yet another John, was created an Earl. An eye for the choice of wealthy heiresses as wives , coupled with a rise in agricultural values, compensated for the decay of the Sussex iron industry which had been their major source of income. In 1840 he married Katherine Charlotte Baillie, and they had seven sons and four daughters.

On his death he was succeeded by his eldest son Bertram (b. 1840) as 5th Earl. Bertram was active in attempting to restore Carlos VII to the Spanish throne and, of course, supported the Catholic church in Battle.

The 5th Earl married Emily Chaplin who died in 1900; he lived until 1913 when he was succeeded by his brother, Thomas, the 6th and last Earl, who was an Anglican and who died without issue in 1924.

Bertram, 5th Earl left a sum of money in his will, which invested in 2 1/2 % stock initially produced £150 pa[78], which was to be paid to the person as priest serving the Battle Mission – see 'The 5th Earl Of Ashburnham's Charity For Church, Presbytery, School And Teacher's House At Battle'[79]. This was not an insignificant sum in 1913.

With the death of the 6th Earl, the direct male line of Ashburnham of Ashburnham (see arms, Fig.51) ended and the title became extinct[80];

77 W. C. Metcalfe, A Book of Knights... (1885), p. 152

78   Victoria County History of Sussex Vol.9 p112
79 http://opencharities.org/charities/280167
80 http://www.cracroftspeerage.co.uk/online/content/index1548.htm

the surviving member of the family was the unmarried and childless Lady Mary Catherine Charlotte Ashburnham (known always as Lady Catherine), daughter of the 5th Earl. She was born 3 January 1890 and died in January, 1953. She could not inherit the estate herself as it was entailed to the nearest male heir.

The estate was passed to the Rev. John Bickersteth on Lady Catherine's death in 1953. As well as huge repair bills he had to pay crippling death duties of £427,000. The contents of the house were sold at auction at Sotheby's in June and July 1953 and half of the estate was sold in the next few years[81].

The house was mostly demolished in 1959, reducing the central section to two floors and the wings to a single story. Meanwhile, John Bickersteth established a prayer centre in the stable block. He gave the remaining parts of the house, and 89 hectares (220 acres) of parkland to the Ashburnham Christian Trust in April 1960. It is now operated as a Christian conference and prayer centre.

Figure 51. The Ashburnham coat of arms

81 http://lh.matthewbeckett.com/houses/lh_sussex_ashburnhamplace.html

Chapter 14
Changes on Mount Street at 'Church Corner' 1700s – 2011

It will be obvious from reading previous chapters and local knowledge of Battle, that the area to the north of Mount Street (previously The Mount) and west of the corner of Mountjoy was and is an area which has seen a lot of the focus of change in the last 300 years. The author has dubbed this area 'Church Corner'. Church Corner continues to change to this day as the Baptist Church extends its Manna House further over the cleared graveyard of the demolished Unitarian chapel.

The diagrams (Figs. 52- 64) below and colour section Figs. C3 and C4 may help the reader understand the changes at Church Corner between the 1700s and 2011.

At first the area was orchards and gardens and sometime before the mid-1600s there existed a drinking house called the Rose and Crown, with a stable, backyard and gardens. In the early 1700s the Presbyterians built, bought or leased a small house to the east of this in 'The Mount'. This house was demolished then on its site (which was expanded by adding half an adjacent orchard) was built a Calvinistic Baptist chapel which would evolve to become a Unitarian chapel. After this a wooden and then an additional more substantial meeting place, Zion Chapel, were built for the Baptists.

In the late 1800s the Unitarian chapel was abandoned and used for other purposes. A Victorian school room was added to the Zion Chapel. Then the Catholic church re-appeared there. The old Unitarian house was demolished in the 1950s. Recently Battle Baptist church has been expanding and building on this reclaimed site.

Figure C3 is a copy of part of the Battle Estate map 1724-1779, with overlays, showing what was probably the old Presbyterian house and the half orchard both purchased by the Independent Calvinists/Baptists in the late 1700s. Together these would become the site of a new Chapel, which would pass to the Universalists at the

138

time of the 1793 split and finally become Unitarian.

A second colour map (Fig. C4) shows the situation as in 1840 on the Tithe Map. On this the Unitarian property is shown outlined in red and the old Rose and Crown land is outlined in cyan. Richard Sinnock had built his own house and garden (on land outlined in cerise) in 1799 and in 1820 given the land outlined in yellow to the Baptists in which to build the Zion Chapel.

The Baptists had built the first Baptist wooden meeting house, which would become their first Sunday School on a small portion of land outlined in orange....which had a pathway with a right of way to it from The Mount (now Mount Street). This building is shown as L-shaped in Fig. C4.

The rest of the original Rose and Crown site passed into others hands and a small playhouse had been erected near the wooden meeting house, sharing its footpath access. Mountjoy did not exist as a road until some time later.

By 1873/79 when a 2500:1 OS map was published (Fig.27) the wooden meeting house had been sold and the Zion Chapel and Unitarian Chapel were co-existing. Sinnock's house was in new private hands. Note that both chapels had a graveyard on this map.

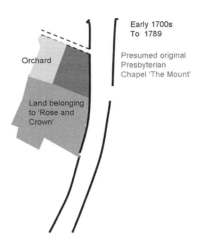

Figure 52. The situation in the early 1700s

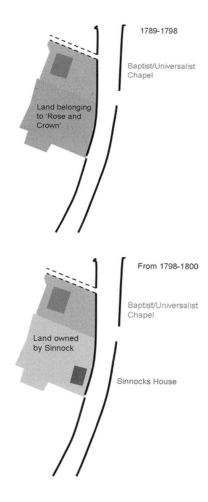

Figure 53. Top diagram: The first Calvinist Baptist chapel is built.

Figure 54. Bottom diagram: Richard Sinnock acquires the land next door

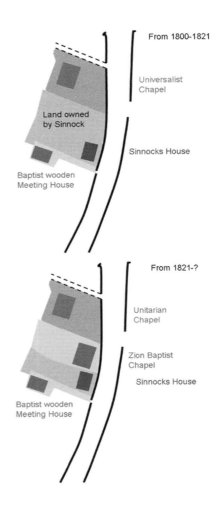

Figure 55. Top diagram: After the split the Calvinist Baptist chapel is kept by the Unitarians and the first Particular Baptist wooden chapel is built on a small piece of land.

Figure 56. Bottom diagram: Richard Sinnock gives land between his house and the Unitarian chapel for Zion chapel to be built

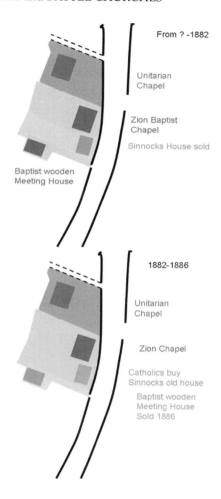

From ? -1882

Unitarian
Chapel

Zion Baptist
Chapel

Sinnocks House sold

Baptist wooden
Meeting House

1882-1886

Unitarian
Chapel

Zion Chapel

Catholics buy
Sinnocks old house

Baptist wooden
Meeting House
Sold 1886

Figure 57. Top diagram: After his death Sinnock's house sold as a separate dwelling

Figure 58. Bottom diagram: Sinnock's old house is bought by the 5th Earl of Ashburnham and the Baptists sell their old wooden meeting house

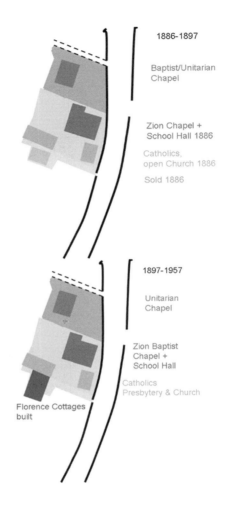

Figure 59. Top diagram: Catholic church and Baptist's Victorian school hall built

Figure 60. Bottom diagram: Florence Cottages built

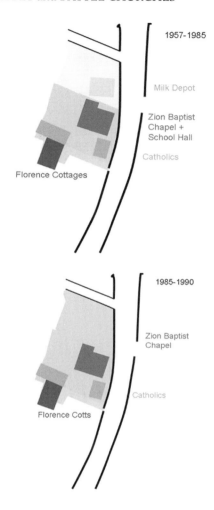

Figure 61. Top diagram: Unitarian chapel demolished and a milk depot is established on its site

Figure 62. Bottom diagram: Baptists buy milk depot site

144

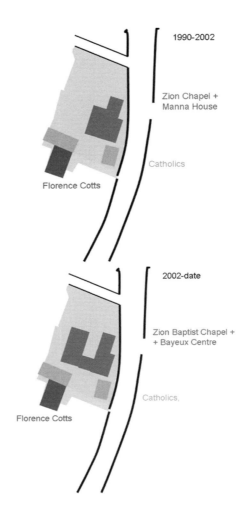

Figure 63. Top diagram: Baptists build Manna House extension

Figure 64. Bottom diagram: Baptists demolish Victorian school hall and build Bayeux centre plus extend Manna House

Chapter 15
A Time-line and the Future of the Churches of Battle 1070 – the Future

The time-line (Fig. C2) shows just how long lived St Mary's Church is. It has existed twice as long as its illustrious founder, the Abbey.

The line also puts into context the relative youth of the more recent Non-conformist Churches which stretch back maximally a quarter of the life of St Mary's. It also shows how long it took for the Catholic Church to become formally re-established in Battle. It also illustrates that churches which do not move with the times and service the needs of their community can close, but that they shall be replaced with those who are more responsive. The map (Fig. C1) shows the positions of the past, present and future churches.

Change continues to occur and is inevitable and to a degree unpredictable. Battle has most of the time accepted this as a liberal community minded town, undoubtedly with a few exceptions, such as those who , when the town cemetery was constructed, asked for separate doors to the Cemetery Chapel - one for C of E members and another for everyone else. At least this was better than in many places where two separate chapels were built! The cemetery chapel is now non-denominational and is run by Battle Town Council. It is available for use on request for both religious and non-religious services.

The impetus for this book was the major change occurring within Battle Methodism. The old Chapel which is Grade 2 listed has been sold and will be converted to other uses. The Methodists have bought some community land just off Harrier Lane on which a new modern Methodist Church and Community Centre will be built to the most modern ecological standards possible. This will be not just a replacement church as its facilities will be open for community use seven days a week.

The wish list has been drawn up and a design template has been chosen and conceptual architectural drawings of the site and the building proposed can be seen below. Final plans will of course await the formal final planning stages, but the group has been keen to use lasting building concepts and also to have modern architectural features which somehow reflect the town of Battle and its surrounding countryside.

Those of us involved with the project hope and pray that it will be a great success for the town as a whole.

The new building is expected to be used by more than one group/organisation at the same time. Therefore discrete spaces/rooms are required:

- Potentially all parts of the building will be available to any group.

- The worship area will be used for other meetings.

- The main hall should accomodate at least 100 sitting and be easily expandable to 160 / 180.

- Designs should flow rather than have 'hard edges'.

- The design, whilst modern, should reflect local features .

- The views from the Centre should maximise the view to the north-east over the local countryside.

- There should be an informal Coffee Lounge with good exterior views and the feel of a 'conservatory';

- There is a need for a 'Quiet Room' – e.g. for use for counselling or prayer.

- Energy saving features shall be considered and used if economically sound. All these items will be evaluated: Solar hot water panels / Photo-voltaic cells / Ground source and Air source heat pumps / heat recovery techniques / biomass boilers / ultra-efficient insulation.

- There should be adequate car parking and disabled access.

- The slope of the site needs to be used to advantage concerning the siting and design of the Centre

Figure C1. Aerial view of Battle with the sites of Churches.
Crosses show active churches. Circles with crosses show demolished or
vacated churches discussed in the book.
Red – C of E   Yellow – Methodists   Magenta – RC Green – Baptists
Orange – Unitarian Cyan – Congregational

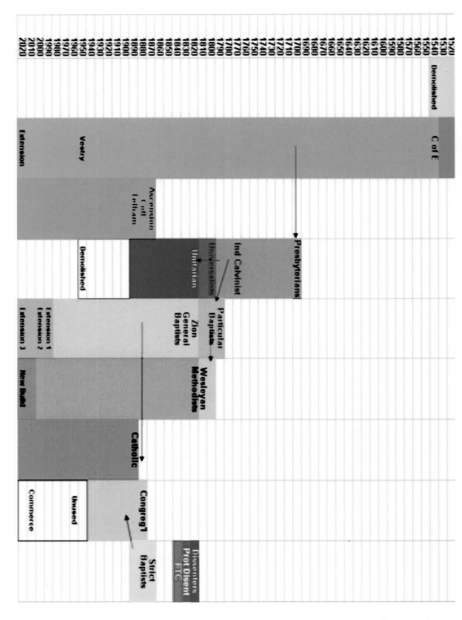

Figure C2

A time-line

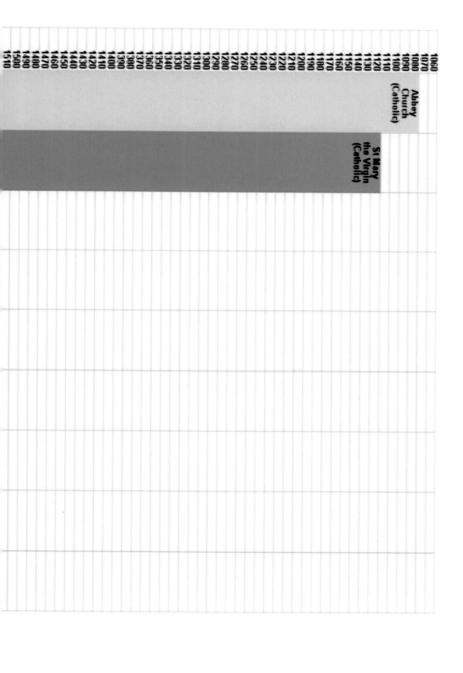

	Abbey Church (Catholic)	St Mary the Virgin (Catholic)
1060		
1070		
1080		
1090		
1100		
1110		
1120		
1130		
1140		
1150		
1160		
1170		
1180		
1190		
1200		
1210		
1220		
1230		
1240		
1250		
1260		
1270		
1280		
1290		
1300		
1310		
1320		
1330		
1340		
1350		
1360		
1370		
1380		
1390		
1400		
1410		
1420		
1430		
1440		
1450		
1460		
1470		
1480		
1490		
1500		
1510		

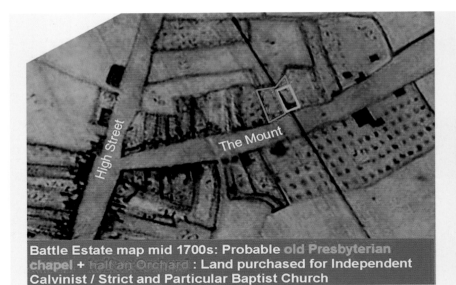

Battle Estate map mid 1700s: Probable old Presbyterian chapel + half an Orchard : Land purchased for Independent Calvinist / Strict and Particular Baptist Church

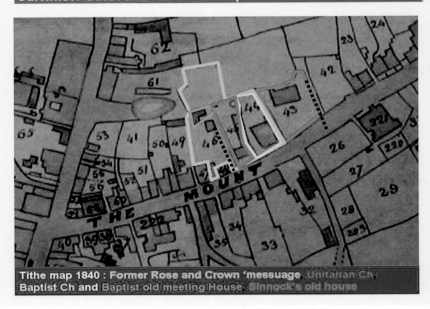

Tithe map 1840 : Former Rose and Crown 'messuage Unitarian Ch. Baptist Ch and Baptist old meeting House Sinnock's old house

Small map sections showing 'The Mount' (Mount Street)

Figure C3. Top : The estate map of Battle Abbey manor mid 1700s

Figure C4. Below : from the 1840 Tithe Map of Battle

Maps © East Sussex Record Office

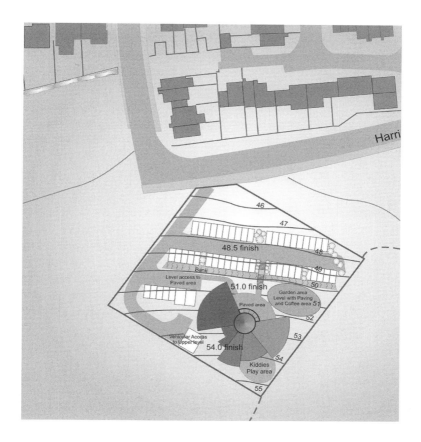

Fig.65. The site of the new Methodist Centre off Harrier Lane. The contour lines demonstrate the slope of the site and the need to have a spilt level building and terraced car parking. (Pinelog Ltd.)

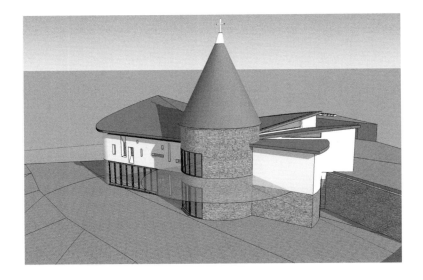

Figure 66

Figure 67

Figure 68

The three figures (66, 67 and 68) above show 3-D pre-contract design thoughts.
The ideas of a tower plus modern 'barns' radiating from this centre are clear. The tower roof concepts await a final choice, as do window details. (Pinelog Ltd.)

The sloped site means that a two layer stepped building is required with retaining walls. A coffee lounge/meeting area, office, toilets and stores as well as the entrance lobby make up the lower level at this stage, cut back into the hillside at the rear. On the upper level a main meeting hall and a secondary meeting room can be combined into one larger space and there is further storage and a lounge / counselling room within the upper level of the tower.
The figures below show the proposed pre-contract floor plans. These confirm that at the rear the upper level is the sole level and that the lower level is cut back somewhat into the slope.

150

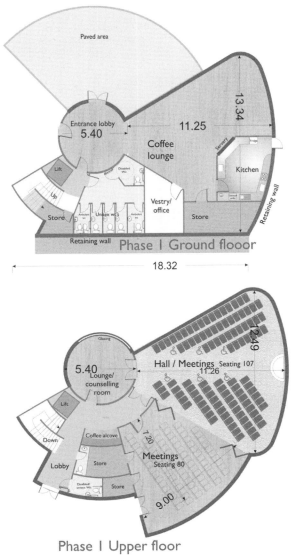

Phase I Ground flooor

Phase I Upper floor

Figures 69 and 70 above show the draft lower and upper floor plans of the first phase of the new Methodist Centre (Pinelog Ltd.). The two meetings rooms are able to be used as one big room. The downstairs lounge will have views to the north and act as a further meeting room.

Battle presently offers places of worship for Christians of four denominations – Anglican, Baptist, Methodist and Roman Catholic – at five Churches. As well as the major changes occurring at the Methodist Church whilst this book is being written, changes are also occurring at other local churches.

Battle Baptists are extending their Manna House. New meeting rooms and toilets are being added at the rear of St Mary's, to be accessed from the Church via the vestry door. The vestry itself was an addition early in the 1900s. During 2011 the tower has been fully re-pointed and belfry beams re-set.

Things do not change just physically but also spiritually. New ideas come and go, good things stay and bad things and mediocrity fail, all that is new is not good, bad or indifferent and neither is all that is old......and spiritual change cannot be imposed, change has to be accepted or it does not happen - or even worse people walk away, exhibiting their disapproval in a physical way. The present Churches of Battle have all moved with the times and modified their approaches to the modern age with an 'open all hours' approach to service the community. No matter what individual beliefs may be, all are welcome.

Appendix

The Surrender of Battle Abbey 1538

This was such an important event for Battle that the various letters and documents that relate to this event and the site's final acquisition by Sir Anthony Browne are reproduced below. These are copied from the work of J. Vidler who himself borrowed from Willis. The originals (mostly in Latin) are of course held in National Archives.

The act for dissolving the great monasteries was passed in 1537-8 (years at that time dated from 25th March in one of our calendar years to 24th March the following year) Below is the instruction from King Henry VIII to the dissolution commissioners to proceed to Battle. It would have been in Latin and dated sometime after February 1538, when the commissioners were sent out

The letter Patent to the commissioners, Gage (Fig. 71) **and Layton.**

"Henry the Eighth &c.

To our Trusty &c. For as much as we understand that the monastery of Battell, is at this present in such state as the same is neither used to the glory of God, nor to the benefit of our common wealth. We let you wit, that therefore being minded to take the same into our own hands for a better purpose, like as we doubt not the head of the same will be contented to make his surrender accordingly ; We for the special trust and confidence that we have in your fidelity, wisdoms, and discretions have, and by these presents do authorize, name, assign and appoint you, that immediately repairing to the said house, ye shall receive of the said head, such a writing under the convent seal, as to your discretions shall seem requisite, meet and convenient, for the due surrender to our use of the same, and thereupon take possession thereof, and of all the goods, catties, plate, jewels, implements, and stuff, being within or appertaining thereunto. And further causing all the goods and implements to be indifferently sold, either for ready money, or days upon sufficient sureties, so that the same pass not one year and a half, ye shall deliver to the said head and brethren, such part of the said money and goods, as ye by your discretions shall think meet and convenient for their dispatch, and further, to see them have convenient pensions by your wisdoms assigned accordingly, which done, and moreover seeing the rightful and due debts thereof paid and satisfied, as well of the revenues as of the said stuff, as to reason and good conscience appertaineth, and your charges reasonably allowed, ye shall proceed to the dissolution of the said house, and further, in your name take possession of the same, to be kept for our use and profit. Ye shall furthermore bring and convey to our tower of London, after your said discretions all the rest of the said money, plate, jewels and ornaments, that in any wise shall come to your hands by means of the premises, or any part thereof, straightly charging all mayors, sheriffs, bailiffs, constables, and all other our officers, ministers and subjects, to whom in this case it shall appertain, that unto you and every of you in execution hereof, they be helping, aiding, favouring and assisting, as they shall answer unto us to the contrary, at their uttermost perils, &c.

Given &c."

Figure 71. Sir John Gage

The commissioners Gage and Layton, arrived at Battel, towards the end of May, 1538.

The following is a translation from the Latin of the actual deed of surrender. Dated 27 May 1538. Reading the above this was clearly a surrender that could not be refused.

"To all the faithful in Christ, to whom the present writing shall come, John, abbot of the monastery of Battell, in the county of Sussex, otherwise called John, abbot of the monastery of St. Martin, of Battell, in the county of Sussex, otherwise called John, abbot of the monastery of Battell, in the county of Sussex, of the order of St. Benedict, and the convent of the same place, health everlasting in the Lord : know ye that we, the aforesaid abbot and convent, with our unanimous assent and consent, deliberate minds, certain knowledge, and mere motion, for certain just and reasonable causes, us, our minds and consciences especially moving, have freely and spontaneously given, granted, and by these presents do give, grant, render, and confirm, to our most illustrious prince and lord, Henry the VIIIth, by the grace of God, of England and France king, defender of the faith, lord of Ireland, and on earth supreme head, all that our monastery or abbey of Battell aforesaid ; and also, all and singular manors, lordships, messuages, gardens, curtilages, tofts, lands, and tenements, meadows, feedings, pastures, woods, rents, reversions, services, mills, passages, knights-fees, wards, marriages, bond-men, villains, with their sequelcommons, liberties, franchises, jurisdictions, offices, courts-leet, hundreds, views of frankpledge, fairs, markets, parks, warrens, vivares, waters, fisheries, ways, passages, void grounds, advowsons, nominations, presentations, and donations of churches, vicarages, chapels, chantries, hospitals, and other ecclesiastical benefices whatsoever, rectories, vicarages, chapels, chantries, pensions, portions, annuities, tithes oblations, and all and singular our emoluments, profits, possessions, hereditaments, and rights whatsoever, as well within the said county of Sussex, as within the counties of Kent, Southampton, Devon, Worcester, Norfolk, Suffolk, Essex, Berks, Oxford, Wilts, Cambridge, as elsewhere within the kingdom of England, Wales and the marches thereof, to the said monastery or abbey of Battell aforesaid, in any wise belonging, appendant, or incumbent ; and all manner, deeds, evidences, writings, muniments in any wise concerning or belonging to the said monastery, manors, lands, tenements, and other the premises, with the appurtenances ; or to any parcel thereof, to have, hold and enjoy the said monastery or abbey, site, grounds, circuit, and precinct of Battell aforesaid ; and, also all and singular lordships, manors, messuages, lands, tenements, rectories, pensions, and other the premises, with all and singular their appurtenances, to our aforesaid most invincible prince and lord the king, his heirs and assigns for ever. To whom, in order to give all the effect of right which can or may thereupon come, we do in this behalf (as is meet) subject and submit ourselves and the said monastery or abbey of Battell aforesaid, and all rights to us, in any wise acquired, giving and granting, to the same royal majesty, his heirs and assigns, all and all manner of full and free faculty, authority and power of disposing of us, and the said monastery of Battell aforesaid, together with all and singular manors, lands, tenements, rents, reversions, services, and every the premises, with their rights and appurtenances whatsoever; and of alienating, giving, converting, and transferring, at his free-will and royal pleasure, to whatsoever uses pleasing to his majesty, ratifying, and by these presents we do promise to ratify, and for ever to confirm such dispositions, alienations, donations, conversions, and translations, to be henceforth by his majesty in any wise made. And, that all and singular the premises may have their due effect, the   elections, moreover, to us and to our successors ; and also all plaints, provocations, appeals, actions, suits, and instances, and all other our remedies and benefits whatsoever, in any wise competent, and hereafter to be competent to us, perhaps, and to our successors in this behalf, by force of the disposition, alienation, translation, and conversion aforesaid, and other the premises. And all exceptions, objections, and allegations of deceit, error, fear, ignorance, or other matter or disposition, being wholly set aside and removed, we have openly, publicly and expressly, and of our certain knowledge, and voluntary inclinations, renounced and yielded up, and by these presents we do renounce and yield up, and from the same do recede in these writings. And we, the aforesaid abbot and convent, and our successors, will warrant the said monastery or abbey, precinct, site, mansion and church of Battell, aforesaid, and all and singular the manors, lordships, messuages, gardens, curtilages, tofts, meadows, feedings, pastures, woods, underwoods, lands, tenements, and all and singular other the premises,with every their appurtenances to our aforesaid lord the king, his heirs, and assigns, against all men for ever, by these presents. In witness whereof we the aforesaid abbot and convent have caused our common seal to be affixed to this writing,

dated the 27th day of the month of May, in the thirtieth year of the reign of our illustrious lord the king."

John, abbot of Battell;

Richard Salehurst, prior;

Clement Westfeld ;

John Henfeld ;

John Hastings, sub prior ;

Thomas Levett ;

Vincent Dunston ;

John Berryng;

Clement Gregory;

Thomas Cuthbert;

William Ambrose ;

Thomas Bede ;

John Jerome ;

Edward Clement;

158

Bartholomew Ciprian;
John Newton;
and Richard Tony.

The seals

The seals affixed to the deed of surrender bear two impressions. The obverse of white wax (Fig.72) represents a large and handsome church, or, according to some opinions, gateway, with a tower and four turrets, within a border in which is the legend, " SIGILLVM CONVENTVS SANCTI MARTINI DE BELLO."

Figure 72. The last seal of the Abbey

The reverse of red wax (Fig.73) has the abbot's seal, which represents a gothic canopy, ornamented with the history of St. Martin, dividing his cloak with the naked beggar. Under the canopy is the figure of a mitred abbot, having his crozier in the right hand, in the other a book : in each of the side compartments is a figure ; one a bishop, the other a female with an olive branch, emblematical of peace; beneath the figures are two shields ; that on the right bearing England and France, quarterly ; that on the left, the arms of the abbey. Gules, a Cross, Or, between four Crowns, Or. Around the whole the legend "Sigil : Johes : dei : gra : de Bello."

Figure 73. The last Abbot, John Hamond's seal

The following letter from the commissioners to lord Cromwell, preserved among the Cottonian Manuscripts. gives us reason to believe that the abbot and monks had prepared themselves for the dissolution of their monastery, by disposing of their most valuable moveable property ; for it cannot be supposed that so rich an abbey was badly provided, after more than four centuries of uninterrupted prosperity, and continually increasing wealth. The accounts of the abbot himself when sacristan shew that new vestments, plate, and other articles were then purchased.

Letter dated 27th May 1538 from the commissioners to Thomas Cromwell. This was in English and the spelling is maintained as was.

" My Lord,
This shal be to advertise yor Lordshippe, that we haue taken the assurance for the kyng, and haue caste or bowke for the dispache of the monks and household, which amownttithe at the leaste to a 2 hundrethe pownds : the implements off the household be the worste that evr I see in Abbaye or Priorie, the vestyments so old and so baysse worn, raggede and torne as your Lordeshipe would not thinke, so that very small money can be made of the vestrye ; if your Lordshippe send us a hundrethe pownds by the bringer we shal make up the reste if hit be possible of the old vestrye stuffe ; if we cannot, we shal disburse y* till or retorne to yr Lordeshipp. The church plate and plate of the household, we suppose by estimation will amount to cccc marks or more: there is no great store of catell; this day we be making an inventorie.

Thus or Lord continewe yowe in honour.
From Battell Abbay, the 27th of May.

Yor Lordshippes to command,
JOHN GAGE
Yor Lordshippes most humble to command,
RICHARD LAYTON PREST.''

The next document dated 6th July 1538 refers to the pensions given to the Abbot, the monks and permanent employees of the Abbey[82]. Information in this document shows that -

The Abbot, by letters patent, dated the 6th of July following, was granted out of the revenues of the monastery, a pension of 100 marks, or £66 13s. 4d.

The sixteen monks who signed the surrender, also had pensions: Richard Salehurst 15 marks or, £10;

Westfeld, Henfeld, Hastings, Levett, Dunstan, Benyng, Gregory, Ambrose, and Bede 10 marks, or 6 13s. 4d. each;

Cuthbert, Jerome, Clement, Ciprian and Dertmouthe, 9 marks, or £6 each.

Willis says that he found no pension assigned to Tony except he be the same with Richard Ladde a novice, whose name is put separate in the Pension Book, in a distinct place after the rest. His allowance was only 4 marks (£2 13s 4d).

A later document dated 1553. shows that pensions were paid to lay employees of the Abbey -

"There remained in charge £26 6s. 4d. in Annuities payable out of the revenues of this convent, besides the ...pensions to ex-monks."

There is also a record in 'Monasticon' that the clerics at the Priory of Brecknock (a cell of Battle) were also pensioned off for the total sum of £29 3s 0d.

Willis in his short account of this abbey and its privileges, says, concerning the destruction.

All which privileges with the Abbey itself coming into King Henry VIIIth's hands at the Dissolution, he soon after, as I was informed when I was at the Place, bestowed the Site of the Church with several of the Lands upon one Gilmer, who for lucre of the Lead, Timber,

---

82 Various books and documents vary between pounds and marks for these pensions. Marks are recorded over the signature of Thomas Cromwell.

&c., in a little time pulled it down and sold the materials; which sacriligious Act thrived not ; for it was soon after sold to Sir Anthony Browne. The church and some other portions of the abbey were destroyed by the authority of the Commissioners, as was the case with many others, and it is probable that Gilmer was the person employed by them to effect the demolition; or he may have given for the materials of the parts to be destroyed, a certain sum, either in "reddy mony or Days upon sufficient Suretyes," and undertaken the demolition at his own cost; in which case he of course, sold the materials to remunerate his outlay.

The portions of the abbey destroyed immediately after the dissolution were the church; the campanile, or bell-tower; the sacristry; the chapter house, which stood on the south side of the choir ; the cloisters ; and perhaps some buildings at the south-east angle of the refectory, and the superstructure of the vaults now remaining : though the latter may have been taken down by Sir Anthony Browne previous to commencing his new buildings which is supposed to have been in 1539.

It is evident from the king's grant to Sir Anthony Browne, within three months after the surrender, that Gilmer never had any part of the place given to him.

The letters patent of 'Henry the VIIIth, dated August the 18th, 1538, granted Battel Abbey, and various of its possessions to Sir Anthony Browne, by the description of

"The site of the late Monastery or Abbey of Battell, in the county of Sussex, then dissolved ; and all the Church, Bell-Tower, and Church-Yard of the said Monastery or Abbey ; also all messuages, edifices, granges, stables, dove-houses, lands, &c., within or adjoining to the site, circuit, or precinct of the same. And one house called the Lodge ; and one garden, and one water-mill called the Park Milne, one lentin called the Tyle-House, and three acres of pasture to the same belonging, in Battell ; also the Great Park, in circuit two miles and a half, and containing by estimation three hundred acres of land, in Battell aforesaid ; and the Little Park, in circuit one mile and a half, and containing by estimation one hundred acres of land ; and also three fields of pasture called Lydbroke, otherwise Sextry, containing by estimation twenty-six acres ; five fields of pasture called Spytel Land, containing twenty-eight acres; one pasture called the Procession Strake ; one small croft of land containing two acres ; one pasture called the Vineyard-Pond, containing seventeen acres ; one pasture called Le Newe ground, containing twenty acres; the Clay Pits, and one other pasture lying without the Butts, containing twenty acres ; one pasture called the Little Maundsy next the end of the garden, containing fifty acres ; one other pasture called the Maundsy next the Butts, containing five acres; the Hay Park of two acres; Cellarers Bayles and the Broom-field, containing sixty acres ; Bellyngfelde of eleven acres ; the New Ground of twenty acres ; and another field called the New Ground, of twenty-two acres ; also a field called the Wek-mede, otherwise Sextry, of fifty acres; two fields called Bencrofte and Stewe-mede, of six acres ; Culvermede, of four acres ; the Long-mede, of ten acres ; Long-mede, of two acres ; the Pasture-fields, ten acres : Almonry-mede, of three acres and a half; three meadows called Spytel-land-meadows, of fifteen acres ; Horse-pond-mede, of five acres ; Marshallmarsh, of sixty-six acres; and all that messuage, grange, and farm, called Bolsham-Felde, containing twelve acres; Hatham-Felde, oftwelve acres; Rolfe-Felde, of six acres ; Petley, of seven acres ; a small field lying near Cornore, of two acres; Hetheboters, of sixty acres; Welland-Felde, of twelve acres; Shepe-Felde, of nine acres and two rods ; Corneore, of twenty-six acres; Marley Pond, of two acres ; three small crofts lying behind Marley Farm House, containing six acres ; Wellande-Mede of twenty acres; Rowland, containing eighteen acres; Seddlescomb-Mede, of twenty acres ; a meadow lying behind the bam of Marley Farm, of sixteen acres ; Cheese-Crofte-Mede, of eight acres ; Barnehorne Pond, situate in the parish of Howe ; and also ten acres, parcel of the manor of Barnehorne, and lying contiguous to the said pond." " Also all, and all manner of tenths whatsoever of all and singular the said premises ; and all tenths of grain and standing corn in the parish or town of Battell. "All and singular which premises above mentioned, are lying and being in Battell, Marley, and Howe, in the county of Sussex ; and belong to the said late Monastery."" Also all the lordship and manor of Battell, with its members and appurtenances, belonging to the said late Monastery ; and the Rectory, advowson, donation, presentation, and right of patronage of Battell ; and all advowsons, &c., of the Vicarage of the parish of Battell ; together with all and singular, messuages, lands, &c., in Battell, Marley, Seddlescombe, Watlyngton, Hertsmonceux, Warkling, Cattesfelde, Tellham,, Ukeham, Swynham, Willingdon, Westdene, Hollyngton, Bexle, Bodyham, and Angmereherst, in the county of Sussex, and in Romney Marsh in the county of Kent, belonging to the said late Monastery ; as fully as they were held by John Hamond, late abbot of the said late Monastery, or any of his predecessors abbots of the same." " To hold to the said Anthony Browne for ever of the King and his successors, in capite, by the service of two knight's fees, and a yearly rent of twelve pounds, in full of all rents, demands, and services whatsoever, &c., &c."

Author's note:

These comprehensive documents and other data leave no doubt that every i was dotted and every t crossed in the documentation leaving no loophole to the events. It was indeed an offer the Abbey and its Abbot could not refuse.

East Sussex at that time was very vulnerable to French attacks and the dissolution of Battle Abbey and the seizure of adjoining lands from Brede to as far as Rye from the Abbaye de Fécamp to the east of Battle would have left a local power vacuum. It is therefore interesting that Henry VIII gave both sets of lands to Sir Anthony Browne who was his trusted friend and could be relied upon to defend the area.

Bibliography/Sources
Books and papers

André J L: Battle Church, SAC 42 (1899) pp214-36

Barnes, K: The Jenner Family's Association with Battle Baptist Church (Zion) 1866-1880, 1995

Boys-Behrens L: Battle Abbey Under 39 Kings, London, 1937

Brakspear H: Battle Abbey, Sussex: An illustrated historical sketch. Reprinted 1950

Braybrooke C: A History of the Parish Church of Battle, 2009

Brewer Rev. J S (Ed.) Anglia Christina Society : Chronicon Monasterii De Bello – original Latin transcript by the Record Office, with English preface and chronological abstract (London, 1854) *see Searle E, below for a modern translation and interpretation*

Browne-Willis: History of Mitred Abbeys, 1718

Butt-Thompson F W and others: The History of The Battle Baptist Church, 1909

Butt-Thompson F W: William Vidler. Baptist Quarterly (17) p3-9, 1957

Carter, A: Chapel of the Ascension, 2001. A typescript history of the Chapel of the Ascension, Telham (Personal Communication)

Clanchy M T: England and its Rulers 1066 – 1272, 1983

Clarke, Catalogue of Muniments of Battle Abbey (London, 1835), in 97 folio volumes.

Coad J G: Battle Abbey East Sussex and the Battle of Hastings, 1984

Connell J M: The Story of an Old Meeting House, 1916

Coote P: Notes on Battle Methodist Church (2010). Personal communication

Cronne HA and Davis RHC (Eds.) Regesta Regum Anglo-Normannorum Vol.3 1135-1154, 1968

Custumals of Battle Abbey 1283-1312 (Camden Society, 1887), New Series, XLI

Davis HWC (Ed.) Regesta Regum Anglo-Normannorum Vol.1 1066-1100, 1913

Davis RHC & Chibnall Marjorie (Ed.): The Gesta Guillelmi of

William of Poitiers, 1998

Denny N & Filmer-Sankey J (Eds.): The Bayeux Tapestry, 1966

Douglas D & Greenaway G W: English Historical Documents 1042-1189, 1961

Duchess of Cleveland: The Battle Abbey Roll (London, 1889), 3 vols.

Dugdale: Monasticon , III (London, 1821)

Elleray D Robert: Sussex Places of Worship. 2004

English Heritage Handbook.

English Heritage Review of Diocesan Churches 2005

Ford W K (Ed.) Chichester Diocesan Surveys 1686 and 1724. Sussex Record Society Vol.78, p250-1, 1994

Garnett G: Conquered England: Kingship, Succession and Tenure 1066 – 1166, 2007

Garraway-Rice R, Godfrey WH(Ed.): Transcript of Sussex Wills. Sussex Record Society. 1935

Godfrey W H: St Mary the Virgin, Battle, SNQ 11 (Feb 1946) pp6-7

Graham R: English Ecclesiastical Studies. 1929

Hare J N: Battle Abbey. The Eastern Range and the Excavation of 1978-1980, 1985

Hinde T (Ed.): The Domesday Book, 1985

Holinshed R: Chronicles of England, Scotland, and Ireland,1577/87

Jenner D and N: Personal communications

Johnson C and Cronne HA Regesta Regum Anglo-Normannorum Vol.2 1100-1135, 1956

Lambarde W: Perambulation of Kent , 1570

Leland J: Collecteana in Six Volumes, 1716. Available as a 2010 reprint.

Lemmon Lt Col C H., DSO.,The Field of Hastings, 1969

Livett G M: Three East Sussex Churches: Battle, SAC 46 (1903) pp69-93

Lower M A: (Trans. from Latin) The Chronicle of Battel Abbey, London 1851. *But see Searle E, below, a more modern and accurate translation and interpretation.*

Matthew D: The Norman Monasteries and their English Possessions, 1979

McLynn F: 1066 - The Year of the Three Battles, 1998

Meads W E: Notebooks on the ancient churches of E.Sussex (10 vols)

Mee A: Sussex, The King's England, 1937

Morillo S (Ed.): The Battle of Hastings: Sources and Interpretations, 1996

Muniments of Magdalen College, Oxford: Inventory of Plate in the Refectory of Battle Abbey, 1420

Page W: Victorian County History of the County of Sussex vol. 2, 1909

Palmer, S: The Nonconformists Memorial. Vol.2, 1775

Paton Sir J Noel: Note on the Sword of Battle Abbey. Proc. Soc. Antiquaries of Scotland. 1873-4

Platt C: The Abbeys and Priories of Medieval England, 1984

Platt C: The Monastic Grange in Medieval England, 1969

Poyntz Wright P: Great Battles: Hastings, 2005

Quartermain W T: The Parish Churches of Sussex. Two bound volumes of drawings dated 1865, but mostly earlier, though some were added down to c1875. They are divided into East (E) and West (W) Sussex (Sussex Archaeological Society Library)

Rouse E C: Wall Paintings in St Mary's Church, Battle, SAC 119 (1979) pp151-60

SAC. Sharpe Collection. 366 drawings of Sussex Churches, done between 1797 and 1809, mostly by Henry Petrie FSA (Sussex Archaeological Society, Michelham Priory)

SAC. Volume of sepia drawings dated 1852-1900, mostly before 1870 (Sussex Archaeological Society Library)

Salzman L F: Victorian County History of the County of Sussex vol.9, 1937

Searle E (Trans. Ed.): The Chronicle of Battle Abbey, Oxford 1980

Searle E: Lordship and Community – Battle Abbey and its Banlieu 1066-1538, Toronto, 1975

Smith R: The life of the Lady Magdalene, Viscountess Montague (1672) - printed in Southern A C (Ed.) An Elizabethan recusant House (1954)

Smith V: Catalogue: Sussex Churches, Lewes, [1980]

Southern Unitarian Magazine 1888, p22 & p122

Stell, C: Nonconformist Chapels and Meeting Houses in Eastern England, English Heritage (2001). [Covers Sussex]

Stenton F: Anglo-Saxon England, 2001

The 'Christian Freeman' of May 1872 p72

The 'Christian Life' of 14 July 1928 pp225-6, 21 July 1928 p230 & p235 and 28 July 1928 p243 & p251

Vere Hodge F: The Parish Church of St Mary the Virgin Battle, Battle, 1953

Vidler J: The hand book to Battle Abbey. 1850

Vidler J (writing as 'A Native'): Gleanings respecting Battel and its Abbey, 1841

Vidler W A: A Short Account of the Planting of the Particular Baptist Church at Battle in Sussex. Reprinted in the Monthly Repository. 1817

Vidler W A: Prefaces for Winchester's A Defence of Revelation etc. 1796

Wilson Fr. A McL: Notes on Battle Catholic Parish (2010) (Personal communication)

Winchester E: 'Dialogues on The Universal Restoration', published in 1788.

Wright R: Religious History and Character of the Late Rev. William Vidler. Monthly Repository. 1817

Youard W W: The Story of Saint Mary's Church Battle, 2nd Ed. Gloucester , 9th ed. revised and brought up to date by F.H. Outram assisted by R.T. Izard, 1972

On-line

http://www.ashburnham.org.uk/

(about the Ashburnham Christian Trust

http://www.battle-abbey.co.uk

http://www.battlebaptistchurch.org.uk

http://www.british-history.ac.uk/

(extensive old records)

http://www.britishlistedbuildings.co.uk

(texts of English Heritage listings)

http://www.domesdaymap.co.uk

http://dove.cccbr.org/home.php
(about bell-ringing)
http://www.english-heritage.org.uk/daysout/properties/1066-battle-of-hastings-abbey-and-battlefield/
http://www25.uua.org/uuhs/duub/articles/williamvidler.html
http://www.nationalarchives.gov.uk/a2a
http://www.newadvent.org/cathen/
(catholic data)
http://www.paintedchurch.org/
 (incomplete illustrated listings and assessments of mediaeval wall-paintings by Anne Marshall)
http://www.roughwood.net/
(church photographs)
http://www.stainedglassrecords.org/
(detailed listings of C19 and C20 glass in most of southern England, including Sussex, compiled by Robert Eberhard)
http://www.sussex.ac.uk/cih/research/dissentingacademies/
http://www.sussex-opc.org/
(on-line Parish Clerk for Sussex)
http://www.sussex-opc.org/ParishDetails/EastSussex/Battle/BattleUnitarian.htm
(for Mrs M J Hadaway's account of the Unitarian Church)
http://www.surman.english.qmul.ac.uk/
(The Surman Index Online, Dr Williams's Centre for Dissenting Studies. Llists Congregational ministers, but earlier non-conformists are also listed until Congregational congregations established)
http://www.sussexparishchurches.org/
http://www.theclergydatabase.org.uk/
 (The Clergy of the CofE -Database)
http://www.theweald.org/
(extensive data about Wealden families)

East Sussex Record Office references
Baptist/Unitarian
NU/3/1-2 Church books; 1769-1845.
NU/3/2/1 Church book containing an account of the growth of an

Independent Calvinist congregation under George Gilbert's influence in 1776 and its subsequent history *1776-1845.*

NU/3/3-4 Appeal for funds and report on the state of the chapel; 1840-1857.

NU/3/5-9 Papers concerning the sale of the chapel and its use by the Mountjoy Institute; 1896-1928.

NU/3/10-14 Papers concerning the history of the chapel; 1872-1999.

NU/3/11 For a history of the chapel with a biography of William Vidler.

NU/3/14 For a history of the Unitarian Church. The founding of the Particular Baptist Chapel in 1780 (and in a later section of the book) its subsequent history to 1796; note of the appointment of J Parker as Deacon, 25 Dec 1780; minutes of church meetings, Jan 1785 - Mar 1808, Dec 1830 - Dec 1831; rules and regulations of the Unitarian Church at Battle, 15 Jun 1823; note of the adoption of Unitarian views by many of the congregation, 1817, and the resulting dissentions, 1822-1824; minutes of church meetings, Jan 1825 - Feb 1829 (including new laws relating to burials in the chapel yard, 1828), Jan 1843 - Nov 1845 (including new rules, 1844); note of repairs to the chapel, nd [1840s].

NU/3/14/1 The General Baptist Assembly Occasional Paper no 25, A History of the Unitarian Church at Battle, Sussex. By Samuel Collier Burgess and Walter Herbert Burgess, 1888, with additional material by Leonard J Maguire, Apr 1999 *1888, 1999.*

NU/3/15-16 Papers concerning the burial ground; 1980-1984.

NU/3/17-18 Papers concerning the proposed sale of the chapel; 1894-1895.

NU/3/18/1 Thirteen letters to Richard Bartram, St Stephens Chambers, Telegraph Street, Moorgate Street, London, concerning the chapel trust and possible sale of the chapel to the Congregational Church or as a reading room

NU/3/18/1 *Dec 1894 - Jul 1895.* Includes letter from C D Badland, 117 Western Road, Lewes, to Rev W Copeland Bowie [British & Foreign Unitarian Association, Essex Hall, Essex Street, Strand, London].

AMS5876 Memoir of Richard Sinnock 1762-1822, a member of the congregation

Methodist

NMB/51 Battle Wesleyan Methodist Church: minutes of Trustees' meetings, 1874-1879; printed trial and quarterly tickets, 1827-1876; minutes of the Revival and General Management Committee, Leaders' meetings, annual society meetings, 1893-1935.

Hastings Circuit, 1822-1836 (NMA/8)

NMA/8/1 Minutes,

NMA/8/2 Accounts,

NMA/8/3 (NMA/8/3/1) Circuit books, schedules and plans,

NMA/8/4 Register of baptisms,

NMA/8/5 Register of deeds,

NMA/8/6 Attendance Registers,

NMA/8/7-10 Miscellaneous

Telham

CHC/3. Dean Crake's Gift : statements CHC/3/2 *1912 – 34*

Congregational

NC/10/1/1 Manual, 1935

Eastern District minutes (NC/10/2)

NC/10/2/1 Aug 1890 - Sep 1909

NC/10/2/2 Nov 1909 - Sep 1931

NC/10/2/3 Jan 1932 - Nov 1960

Ashburnham Estate

ASH Covering dates 1048 – 1984

Catholic

CHC/3/2 1912 – 1934

CHC/3/3 1923 – 29. Earl of Ashburnham gave money in his will proved 13 Feb 1913

West Sussex Record Office references

(Ecclesiastical documents relating to all the Diocese of Chichester churches, including those of East Sussex etc. are kept at WSRO, not ESRO)

Ep II/25/3 Registrations of Dissenting meeting houses

Ep II/27/266 All documents relating to the 1867/68 restoration of St Mary's, including architectural drawings attributed to W Butterfield are kept under this file series.

PD 2011-14 Tracy, Adelaide: Sussex Churches. Four bound volumes of drawings by Adelaide Tracy and other ladies, dated 1848-57, with photographs, printed material and notes (also known as the Borrer Collection).

Public Record Office – National Archives

Prob 11/1737 Will of Richard Sinnock

Alphabetical Index

184

186